SIN

Hugh Connolly

New Century Theology

CONTINUUM
The Tower Building, 11 York Road, London SE1 7NX
370 Lexington Avenue, New York NY 10017-6503

First published 2002

British Library Cataloguing-in-Publication Data
A catalogue record for this book is available from the British Library.

ISBN: 0-8264-5184-5

Typeset by Kenneth Burnley, Wirral, Cheshire
Printed and bound in Great Britain by Biddles Ltd, Guildford and King's Lynn

Contents

Introduction v

1 Echoes and Resonances in Early Civilizations 1

2 The Biblical Context: God's Unfolding Story of Love 21

3 The Development of the Vocabulary and the Theology of Sin 41

4 Rediscovery, Renewal and Revitalization 63

5 Of Human Fault, Frailty and Finitude 83

6 Solidarity in Sin: The Social Dimension 103

7 Overcoming Sin: Conversion and Reconciliation 125

8 Towards a Synthetic Account of Sin 147

Index 167

Introduction

> What is sin? Does the word have meaning anymore? I have found no agreement about the notion of sin even among those most given to their studies. Always wondering whether this or that is a sin, why it is a sin and when, such things are the real Christian obsession. (Ignatius of Loyola)

These reflections, first voiced by the great soldier-saint almost five centuries ago, still have a very real resonance today at the dawn of the third Christian millennium.

Despite its much-heralded demise, and disagreement as to what exactly sin is, the word continues to have some currency in the modern world. Like all currencies it has of course been susceptible to a little inflation over the years. Whereas it was once exclusively linked with *homo religiosus* and spiritual and theological reflection, sin now seems just as likely to adorn the headlines of newspapers, the scripts of soap operas and the confessions of chat-shows as it did once the pages of prayer books and the handbooks of moral theology. To the popular mind sin at its most crass is akin to the sleazy and salacious, it is the stuff of Soho, Pigalle, Amsterdam and Bangkok. The 'sins of the flesh' are as prevalent as ever, but nowadays they are big business – and, what's more, they sell newspapers.

In its adjectival form the term enjoys a somewhat more

refined existence. The 'sinful' has become something of a synonym for life's little luxuries: gourmet food, designer clothes, refined perfumes, deluxe automobiles. 'Sinful' products are for people who like to pamper themselves knowing that 'they're worth it' after all. So in answer to the question once memorably posed by the psychologist Karl Menninger, 'Whatever became of sin?' one might reply that nowadays it has become a victim of its own success, it has grown old and fat and has lost its teeth!

In more theological terms, one could say that the language of sin has become somewhat ineffectual in terms of its ethical and religious meanings. There is a lack of vitality and freshness and resonance with reality. No doubt theology itself must shoulder a share of the blame here. For generations, sin had been trussed up into something of a philosophical straitjacket which left it ill-equipped to deal with the real moral issues of the mid-to-late twentieth century. Engaged and intrigued by the newly emerging data and research of the human sciences, contemporary Christians found their understanding of sin incapable of speaking to their new self-understanding and unable to address a plethora of fresh moral issues. Sin had become all but meaningless in a modern world and had little or nothing of value to say to ordinary life.

And yet the experience of frailty and moral failure remained. Despite the valuable work of psychologists in uncovering the psychic inhibitions that impede moral growth and in unmasking the guilt feelings which arise from the ego there was awareness that psychology could not simply explain sin away without at the same time destroying the very idea of human freedom. There was a recognition too that, despite the psychic, societal, familial and cultural influences which shape our growth and development, human beings still possessed a very real capacity to choose between good and evil. They could decide whether to espouse an approach to life that is life-giving or else to adopt an attitude which is self-centred and selfish and disregards the needs and concerns of others.

Our aim in this little volume therefore has been not so much to unearth dramatic new insights into a question, which has, after all, been well explored for centuries and indeed millennia; we have sought here instead to draw on the vast and valuable store of biblical and historical material which may now, in a new theological climate, be ready for rediscovery and re-formulation in a more synthetic way. But we must beg the reader's patience in this regard if the approach in the first half of the book appears to be somewhat slavishly historical. It is neither the author's intention nor competence to give a history lesson. Rather, this approach has been taken out of the awareness that there are key moments in our tradition's theological engagement with sin which are deserving of exploration and a realization that sometimes the most vigorous growth emerges from seeds that have long lain dormant.

The time may be ripe therefore for a more holistic and integrated account of sin in the light of significant changes of emphasis in the Church's self-understanding and of a new and more profound awareness by Christians of the dynamic nature of their relationship to God.

Indeed, the terms 'dynamic', 'integral' and 'synthetic' are keys to the enterprise being undertaken here. On the one hand, it has become evident that catalogues of infringements and violations of laws, no matter how comprehensive, no longer do justice to the seriousness of the *mysterium peccatis*. On the other hand, at a more figurative level the imagery that we use to reflect on sin is multiple and varied and there is awareness that no one insight can capture the fullness of meaning.

When one surveys the vast literature which has been given over to the analysis of sin, guilt, evil and so forth, one cannot but be reminded of the humorous Indian fable about the three blind men who came across an elephant. Each variously described the unfortunate beast as resembling a rope, a tree or a spear depending on whether he has seized its tail, trunk or tusk. Perhaps, like the elephant, there are also aspects of the mystery of human sin and evil which will forever elude us. Paradoxically, the question of sin, at another level, provides a point of contact for strands of thought from many different fields. Sociological 'anomie', philosophical 'angst', economic 'alienation', political 'apathy' and even biological 'ailment' all seem to find a resonance in the doctrine, the phenomenon and the experience which Christians have traditionally called sin. No doubt practitioners of each of these disciplines would dispute which concept is the real matrix and the more central to what it means to be human.

Be that as it may, it is the intent of this book to show that the idea of sin is capable of shedding light and meaning on all aspects of human existence. For that reason it will be argued that it is most appropriately considered in the context of the overall vocation to become fully human and fully children of God. Far from being an oppressive religious construct, we will make the case that precisely because sin affects human beings at every level of their existence, it also draws their attention to the grandeur of the human calling. Sin is therefore just the other side of grace, of that supernatural dynamic which is at work within the human heart, transforming each person into an incarnation of love, and into a living reflection, in thought, word and deed, of the One who is love.

1

Echoes and Resonances in Early Civilizations

> Was I the sinner?
> Repaying wrong for wrong – that was no sin?
> Even were it wittingly done as it were not
> I did not know the way I went. (Oedipus at Colonus)

While very much a part of the Judaeo–Christian worldview, the idea of sin has nevertheless significant resonances in many religions, not least within some of Israel's neighbouring cults and cultures. At one level the awareness of wrongdoing is of course a basic human intuition strongly linked to the consciousness of guilt, to the phenomenology of evil and to the interplay between human responsibility and religious and cultic practices.

In Egypt, for instance, the idea of an 'after-death judgement' was already in vogue 2,000 years before the time of Christ. The so-called 'Book of the Dead' evoked a kind of tribunal where the heart was 'weighed in the balance' in order to ascertain what good or evil the deceased person might have been responsible for during their lifetime. The tribunal allowed for the soul to make its case, to review the sum of deeds (both good and ill) which had been carried out over the course of a lifetime and to ask for justice on the basis of these deeds.

> I did no evil thing . . . I did not do that which the god abominates. I did no murder, I caused no man misery, I did not commit adultery; I am purified four times; there arises no evil thing against me in this land, in the hall of truth.[1]

The idea that the actions and deeds which were accomplished throughout one's life might one day be assessed and reviewed by the deity after death belonged to the earliest period of Egyptian civilization and continued to hold for many generations. Unlike the Christian idea of a 'Day of Judgement' which would concern all humankind more or less simultaneously, the Egyptians believed instead in an individual judgement where the fate of the soul would be decided. The possibilities were only two: either total destruction or else permission to enter the kingdom of Osiris and the Blessed. A clear distinction was made between those adjudged to be wicked and the remainder who were pure and blessed.

So in or around 3600 BC the idea of an end-of-life 'weighing up' process had already been more or less established. The religious schools of Egypt had by this time assigned to a particular god the guardianship or task of monitoring the balance during the trial of souls. The god was to oversee the weighing process lest any foul play prejudice the final judgement of the soul. But there was no suggestion here of forgiveness; the final verdict was simply the automatic consequence of the review of life. Still less was there, as yet, any real sense of personal responsibility; indeed, the trial was believed to be witnessed by the *Shenit*, those supernatural beings who were thought to control the acts and deeds of human beings. In the end, if the deceased person were deemed to have found favour in the 'great weighing', judgement might be pronounced along the following lines: 'The heart has been weighed, and his soul has stood as a witness for him, it has been found true by trial in the Great Balance. There has not been found any wickedness in him."[2]

The Babylonian peoples, unlike the Egyptians, were not only aware of their sin but devised means of expressing their sense of personal guilt and need of forgiveness. Sin, all the same, tended to be construed here in a naturalistic rather than a moral sense. More often than not, it was believed to have manifested itself in some sort of illness and as a result was attributed to a demon. At the onset of the illness the Babylonians would take themselves to their priest or exorcist to seek reconciliation with heaven. It was essential to have sin taken away because, once freed from sin, the individual would never again be abandoned by their God and evil could have no power over them. The priest-exorcist would then proceed to confess his penitent without requiring a very detailed confession. He would instead enumerate all known sins capable of being committed. Throughout the process the penitent would remain silent, for the listing of sins was not so much an interrogation of the sinner as a prayer to the deity. Beginning with the sins of the tongue – thought to indicate a lack of openness or an injustice or foul play – the priest would then move on to faults against the godhead, neglect of parents, false transactions and the like. This would be followed by transgressions of boundaries such as entering another's house, making an objectionable approach to another's wife, spilling another's blood, or stealing another's garment. After this there would follow a further litany dealing with such matters as false teaching, practice of sorcery or magic and breaking one's word.

There was also a significant category dealing with mistakes in the cult and worship, which included drinking from an impure source, swearing to God with unwashed hands, eating the sacrificed food and even urinating or spitting in a river! To our mind, this mixing of moral failures with liturgical faults may appear to be more than a little bizarre. (We have only to read some of the Penitential books, though, to see similar instances of this in the Christian tradition.) We should bear in mind that in religions such as that of the Babylonians, which entailed an external cult, liturgical slip-ups were a serious matter because they were seen as a direct offence to the deity. Sins against the common good were also serious – interfering with the water supply or denying it to another, speaking against the interests of the village, uprooting crops or hunting game which was too young – all of these were deemed grave transgressions.

Even after reciting this lengthy list of faults the exorcist could not yet rest for there was still the possibility that the 'sin' had been incurred not by one's own hand but 'by association', as it were. He would therefore have to enquire whether his 'client' had slept on the bed of an evil spirit or sat on his seat, or eaten from his plate, or drunk from his cup, was warmed by his fire, and so forth. The next question would investigate whether the source of evil was an animate being: one's father, mother, brother, sister, neighbour, living persons, dead persons, those known or unknown, a man, a woman or even a child. Next would come a review of the likely place of contamination – the entrance to the town, the doorway, the bazaar, the temple, or the roads.

Eventually, having thoroughly recounted all of these possibilities, the exorcist would formally seek the assistance of the gods and would embark upon an equally lengthy litany of invocation. In this way he would beseech the gods, the winds, the stars, the waters, to pardon the sin and thus break the spell of evil. Sometimes a symbolic ritual was enacted such as the burning of an object in order to provoke the 'combustion' of sin according to a particular given formula. A typical formula ran:

> As this onion is peeled and thrown in the fire and consumed by the great burning *Gibil* so that it will no

> longer be planted in the furrow, its roots no longer dug into the earth, its stem will no longer thrust upward. It will never again see the sun, nor be placed on the table of a god or a king. So too may the curse, the pain, the suffering, the fault, the illness, the offence, the crime, the sin, the fault, the malady which is in my body, my flesh, my members be peeled as this onion. May the burning *Girru* consume it today. May the spell disappear and may I see the light![3]

Given his extraordinary and supernatural powers the exorcist also played an official role in the consecration of kings. He was the 'enemy of demons' and therefore charged with the expiatory ritual, which was an important component of any consecration ceremony. This ritual commenced with several fumigations by incense and purifications with water, fire and herbs. The exorcist would dress in sombre colours and would erect seven altars in the courtyard of the palace. A lamb would be brought and slaughtered, and after various other rites the king would ask pardon for his 'sins'. The blood of the slain lamb would then be taken and sprinkled on the lintels of the palace doorway.

It is difficult not to find oneself making some associations between this practice and the later Passover rites of the Jews, or indeed to suggest a common ancestral link with Christian notions of sacrifice as atonement for and expiation of sin. There is also a view that the Babylonians may already have had the idea of 'wiping away' fault. The term *Kippuru*, used to describe the priest or exorcist, is in fact an antecedent and cognate of the Old Testament *kipper* which indicated wiping away or blotting out or making disappear. (The expression is largely the same as that readily recognized by us today in the name of the Jewish feast, *Yom Kippur*.)[4] But such an action in a Babylonian cult would most likely have been more simply understood as a charm to ward off the attentions of demons and would not therefore have had strictly expiatory connotations. In any event, and whatever the truth of such speculation, it is apparent that the Babylonians had a relatively sophisticated understanding of fault, which though largely pre-ethical and naturalistic was holistic in its emphasis and expression. At the same time the underlying ideas are very pessimistic. Human beings fall into sin by virtue of their very existence. 'The free will of men is never quite up to the divine standards of purity.'[5]

The Greek notion of sin was somewhat different. The great classical works of literature tend to portray sin as 'overstepping the prescribed limits'. For many of the great dramatists and poets sin was essentially an inordinate emphasis on the self. It consisted in self-seeking or self-assertion, accompanied by overweening arrogance and pride. The tragic theatre and its preoccupation with the patterns of human passions and fallibility became a notable medium for reflection on human guilt and responsibility. Human existence was represented here as being easily prone to becoming trapped in the quicksand of *hubris* and *ātē*, that terrible and delusional cocktail of pride and power, which would seize upon individuals and eventually bring about their ruin.

Their great tragedians and thinkers struggled with the ultimate problems of guilt and fate and the repercussions of mistaken and 'sinful' choices. The *Persae of Aeschylus* for instance ascribed the failure of the Persians to become a great Western power to their 'transgression of the bounds', which the gods had fixed to their empire – and because of this, mastery of the sea was never to be theirs. Euripedes, in turn, perplexed before the vastness of human sin, exclaims: 'if Zeus were to write the sins of men – the whole heaven would not suffice'.

In a more systematic reflection on the nature of moral failure, but without exploring the religious connotations, Aristotle outlined three separate categories of human fallibility: *kakía* (vice), *thēriotēs* (moral insensitivity) and *akrāsia* (moral incontinence). *Kakía* he described as a kind of failure to 'hit the mark' or find the goal, which for him consisted ultimately in seeking the virtuous mid-path between opposing evils. *Thēriotēs*, by contrast, is a kind of dulling of the moral sense whereby the individual is incapable of knowing how to choose the good. Both concepts were considered by the great philosopher to be a failure of intelligence.

On the other hand, the third concept, *akrāsia*, pointed to something much deeper. It described the state of human beings that did not, for one reason or another, live the 'life of reason' which was to be achieved through right training and experience and which led to the skills of foresight and intelligence. Aristotle believed that human beings were capable of knowing the intelligent thing to do but often failed to do it owing to what he called 'moral incontinence', or in other words a lack of self-control.

For Homer, on the other hand, the gods were always active but even the gods were subject to the power of *moira* (fate). This was not simply predetermination. Certainly fate could include evil, but one could also bring more evil upon oneself through one's action or indeed inaction. Certain behaviours and attitudes were frowned upon because they were deemed shameful in themselves. Some things just were not done: perjury, incest, and violation of hospitality. The ethical framework here was in fact what has come to be known as a 'shame culture' as distinct from the 'guilt culture' to be found in the Jewish and Christian notions of sin.[6] In short, there is 'more fascination in Greece with hero worship than with hamartology . . . The Homeric hero loses face and his reputation which means everything to him.'[7]

Orphism and Sophism, the so-called Mystery religions, Stoicism, and later religious phenomena in the Greco–Roman world, are also instructive. Their conception of sin and death makes a particularly interesting contrast with the classical

Greek view. The Greeks held that the human soul had no pre-existence before physical birth and only a shadow existence after death. Homer's *Iliad*, for instance, opens with a reference to 'the souls which are hurled down to Hades'. To the Greek mind, Hades was a mere fact of life (or rather death) in which it was believed one had a kind of shadow existence. Death led neither to reward nor punishment – merely transition to a new kind of existence that was but a pale reflection of the life which went before. Conversely, for Orphism, which had its origins in the sixth century BC and finds a voice in the poetry of Pindar, the soul is quite distinct from the body. Indeed, the body may in some sense be seen as the 'tomb of the soul'. Only asceticism can help to liberate the soul from the physical impurity of the body, and where this is not done one may have to pay for one's sins in the after-life. One example of this kind of thinking was to be found in the Asclepius cult. Asclepius – god of the physicians – was presented as the most sympathetic of the gods. He was a god who cured the sick, and even on occasion raised the dead. Some latter-day scholars have described him as the most 'Christ-like' of the pagan deities because of his sympathy for human suffering and his capacity for loving action. Nonetheless, even Asclepius could not heal those who were not themselves virtuous. The inscription above the entrance to his shrine read 'Pure must be he who enters the fragrant temple, purity means to be wise in holy things.'[8]

The Asclepius cult of course didn't have anything approaching a systematic account of sin, but there is to be found there an affirmation of the link between what is done in this life and that to be enjoyed in the next. A connection is also made here between sickness and moral imperfection on the one hand, and healing and wholeness on the other. Unusually, Greek thought makes a direct if undeveloped link here between the 'moral life' and the after-life. The link is a tangible one. It is rooted in the raw material of human morality – sin on the one hand and virtue on the other. In this way Orphism attempted to deepen its understanding of the human condition.

Later, the Sophists and poets such as Aristophanes and Euripides were also to challenge traditional religious mindsets and assumptions. Whereas Homer, for instance, saw no reason to question the sexual affairs of Zeus (he considered these not to be a question of lust but simply a divine prerogative to bring order into the divine society), Euripedes and the Sophists began to reflect rationally on the gods and their behaviour and even to challenge and critique their moral conduct. He once remarked: 'If the gods do anything shameful, they are no gods'.[9] In this way the ground was perhaps gradually being prepared for a new understanding of fault and wrongdoing.

The so-called 'mysteries' – ancient fertility rites and religious practices and cults which sought to bring the individual into a special relationship with the deity – were another rich source of reflection on the phenomenon of fault and failure. These were classified into the 'local' and the 'universal'. Among the better known of the universal mysteries were those of Dionysius and Mithra, as well as of the aforementioned Egyptian gods, Osiris and Isis. There is some evidence there of a grappling with and aspiration toward practices of atonement and penance. The devotees of Isis, for instance, had a well-established practice of taking up position outside her temple, from where they bemoaned their sins aloud as they carried out acts of penance.[10]

Another of the mysteries – namely that of the 'Mother of the gods and the Cabiri' at Samothrace – included sacrificial rites and patterns of purification, including a 'rigid enquiry into the sins of candidates'.[11] Apparently this 'local' mystery religion had, for all intents and purposes, a rudimentary foreshadowing of confession of sins. In a not dissimilar way the priests of the Syrian goddess Alagartes would wander throughout the countryside proclaiming their sins aloud and often flailing themselves with whips.

Speculation on any eventual transference or influence between the so-called mysteries and the rites of the Judaeo–Christian tradition is, of course, little more than conjecture, but awareness of these practices can be helpful in sketching a map of the slowly evolving human understanding of sin. That said, the notion of sin that one is dealing with here is at best a very primitive one. Unlike Christianity, it is not linked to any kind of moral conversion or to a supernaturally sanctioned ethic.

Perhaps the closest parallel to real moral conversion is to be found in Mithraism. The Mithraic religion, which may have had its roots in Persia, appears to have evolved a doctrine of moral progression and ascent through various grades of perfection. Often represented artistically by symbolic lions breathing purificatory fire and burning incense, the followers of this cult saw in the scented flames an image of the human body which would one day be consumed and would pass through the purification of flames in its ascent to the heavens.[12] In some respects there was a simple if basic reflection here on the enigma of the human condition and on the manner in which one might escape its limitations.

At another level still of religious sophistication it is believed that the Stoics held the following propositions to be essential dogmas:

1. that the gods exist;
2. that they are benevolent and immortal;
3. that they govern the universe; and
4. that they seek the good of humankind.

In affirming these ideas the Stoics turned their backs for ever upon belief in gods who were greedy, jealous, mischievous or haughty. The whole atmosphere of Stoic religion was therefore quite alien to that in which the gods of the Greek and Roman mythology had taken root.[13] The fact that the gods willed the good of humankind implied that human beings for their part had to act in accordance with the divine will. 'So live, says the Stoic leader, with your fellowmen, as believing that God sees you, so hold converse with God as to be willing that all men should hear you.'[14] And to assist them in this aspiration, human beings were required to examine their souls daily to ascertain whether they were in tune with 'the purposes of the universe'. Thus Seneca could advise 'how beautiful is the custom of reviewing the whole day! How quiet a sleep follows in self-examination. The mind takes its place in the judgement seat, investigates its own actions, and awards praise or praise according as they are deserved'.[15] The soul considered in this way was seen to be evolving toward either, on the one hand, a just and kind sovereign, or on the other a greedy and ungovernable tyrant (Ep. 114, 24). The soul was potentially a font of goodness or a seat of evil.

But for the Stoics, sins were not to be punished by hellfire. 'Ignorance of philosophy,' says Cicero, 'has produced the belief in hell and its terrors.'[16] Seneca in turn dismissed the notion with the advice that 'these tales which make the world below terrible to us are but poetic fictions'.[17]

The idea of some sort of purgatory did find a resonance, nevertheless, with the Stoics. Seneca, for instance, invited his friends to look forward to a period of purgation where the soul would begin its process of refinement before ascending to the tranquil and blissful home in the 'clear bright ether'. The blessed soul, having cast off the 'burden of the flesh', would have the opportunity in its purged state to enjoy free converse with the 'great ones of the past and gaze down at the human world below'. Here again, at first glance, parallels with later Christian beliefs may seem quite obvious, but the observer must tread carefully. The description of death as casting off the 'burden of the flesh' in fact holds the real key to the Stoic purgatory. Death is therefore not so much a cleansing of sins, or even punishment for past offences. It is instead a necessary means for the purification of the soul from the taint of its long contact with the body. The Stoics had, after all, a dualistic conception of human nature where the body was considered to be, in a sense, the 'prison-house' of the soul. The purgation period saw the separation of the soul from the human body, the incorporeal from the corporeal.

Of course, early Christian writers, notably St Paul, were in due course to take up this notion of the 'burden of the flesh' and see in it a metaphor for sin and human frailty. In so doing they were able to tap into a rich seam of thought which was already familiar to the Greco–Roman mind. It may be, though, that this was done at the expense of importing some of Stoic dualism into Christian theology. Arguably, this dualism has bedevilled certain areas of Christian ethics, notably the theological reflections on marriage and human sexuality, ever since. Notwithstanding this observation we must allow that Stoicism did still have in itself a conception of sin as a lack of knowledge, a lack of moral tone and a lack of healthy dispositions in the soul. Three ideas in particular emerge here: *hamartia* – missing of the mark at which virtue aims; *peccatum* – stumbling on the road to virtue; and *transilio* – transgression of appropriate boundaries. But sin, by and large, still has its roots in ignorance and false knowledge. And it was considered the particular task of philosophy to overcome this ignorance. In so doing it had to overcome sinful conditions such as 'fear, greed, grief and excitement'. The aim was to achieve a 'passive character' which bore the virtuous hallmarks of endurance, patience and restraint. 'Bear and forbear' would be the motto of the good Stoic as well as the recipe for a healthy soul.

For the Stoics, indeed, the language of sin or vice was descriptive of a 'sickness of the soul'. Soul sickness could be of varying intensity, and at least three gradations were suggested. The first was a 'ruffling' or slight disturbance, the second an infection or illness, the third, full-blown disease, corresponded to ingrained vice. But virtue was never fully uprooted, and with perseverance, discipline and training it could again blossom and in time transform the 'health' of the soul once more.

This kind of conversion process from the 'ever-present dangers of sin', as described by some Stoic cults, has a decidedly Christian ring to the contemporary ear. 'You carry God about with you, you carry him within yourself, and you profane him, without being aware of it, by impure thoughts and unclean actions'.[18] Similarly Seneca: 'we shall ever be obliged to pronounce the same sentence upon ourselves, that we have been evil and (I will add reluctantly) shall be evil. Every vice exists in every man though every vice is not prominent in each . . . not one of us is without fault'.[19] Likewise, Antoninus observes: 'to be unjust is to sin, to lie is to sin, to seek pleasures as good or to shun pains as evil is sin' because 'he who transgresses the will of nature sins, to wit, against the primal Deity'.[20] This is still a long way, of course, from the idea of sin as an offence against the holiness and the love of a personal God, such as are to be encountered in both the Old and New Testaments. Nevertheless, when it comes to a philosophical and indeed theological reflection on human fault and failure, Stoicism could be said to have successfully stated some of the ethical problems which surround human weakness, and to have even begun to pave a path toward their resolution.

A final grouping of antecedent cults and culture worthy of some attention, because of the later role that the Church in the Celtic lands was to play in the development of penitential theology, is the religious, civil and cultural 'umbrella' now referred to as Druidism. Although Druidism was named by Aristotle[21] as one of the important links in the development of philosophy, it remains to this day one of its least-known systems. In some respects Druidism, like Stoicism, seems to have unwittingly prepared its adherents for an acceptance of Christianity.[22]

There is very little record though of the spirit of druidic religion. From the fragmentary evidence that does exist, however, we see them as seekers after God who were linked by strong ties to the unseen and were eager to conquer the unknown by religious rite or magic art and to pass on their ways to subsequent generations. For this reason the training of druidic students was, it seems, a lengthy and demanding process. Some of the Roman authors describe them as a people who welcomed authority in religion and who were anxious not to transgress the law of the gods.[23]

There is little evidence of any universal ethical teaching in Druidism. Their belief in re-birth may seem to have echoed in some respects the Pythagorean doctrine, but it also differed considerably in that there was certainly no suggestion that re-births could be understood as punishment for sin.

Some forms of Druidism, notably those in Gaul, do seem all the same to have evolved quite sophisticated ethical reflections. A recent study, for instance, notes a series of ethical rules, which was drawn from the bardic triads and on the druidic predilection for 'triplism'. According to this doctrine the laws of the universe were believed to conform to a threefold structure. Three rules had to be adhered to in order to ensure harmony between mortals and the divine, namely: adore God, do no wrong to anyone, act justly to everyone. Druids knew three great fears: offending God, contravening the love of another, and unduly accumulating riches. There were also three vices: pride, hatred, and cupidity, as well as three duties: to love, to create, and to learn; and three virtues: knowledge, love, and courage.[24]

It is difficult, of course, to draw any but the most banal parallels between Druidic understanding of fault and blame, and the Christian concept of sin. But the role of the Druids themselves may well have made something of a later impact on evolving Christian rituals of repentance and confession. The Druid has been variously described as 'shaman, priest, poet, philosopher, physician, judge and prophet' and as exercising a function akin to a 'court-chaplain'. In pre-Christian Ireland, for instance, they were said to be advisers, confidants and chief justices to the High Kings.[25] Celtic Christianity in monastic form gradually supplanted any remnants of Druidism. The monastic tradition of 'soul-friend' also inevitably replaced the older role of Druidic counsellor, but, like all missionary developments, some of the hallmarks of the old were inevitably taken up, adapted and re-presented in the new. The Christian practice of auricular confession of sins to a spiritual director may well, in time, have developed out of the soul-friend or *anamchara* tradition – a tradition that, it is thought, could still have borne some distant resonances of the predecessor culture.

By way of concluding and summarizing this brief overview of some early foreshadowings of sin, one might venture that the Egyptian and Babylonian notions of sin were more a characteristic of religion than of ethics, whereas the converse was true of Hellenistic thought. There needn't, of course, be any automatic opposition between the two. It may in fact prove helpful for us here to think of religion and morality as two different but not opposing forms.

Ethics, to the classical mind, was a way of rationalizing human life and reality. As such, it encapsulated religious expression and assigned a particular role to this area of human experience. Sin for their philosophers was ethical sin: it was transgression of the law or failure to carry out one's duty. On the other hand, it seems that even for the Greeks the purely rational approach was in itself insufficient. Like the Babylonians, Egyptians and the Celts they sought some further form of religious self-expression to profess their experience of inadequacy and of dependence on the gods.

More fundamentally, there were here the beginnings of another understanding of sin, a sense of the profane, a sense of lack, of something that was amiss in the human condition and which separated humanity from the gods. It was an articulation, in other words, of an awareness of human ignorance. To the Greek mind, sinful acts were, as we have said, largely the result of ignorance. Even actions which bore all the hallmarks of malicious deeds, could be attributed to fate or to the conspiracy of the gods. The individual thereby became, in a sense, the 'plaything of divine caprice'. This of course was to become the very essence of classical tragedy, where the human being was ultimately seen to be at the mercy of the gods. The 'mysteries' likewise, while diverging considerably from the classical mentality, stopped short of developing a sense of personal responsibility in the Judaeo–Christian way. Their tendency to view sin and evil as being associated with matter, that is to say still extrinsic to human will, did not allow for any real engagement with the idea of ethical accountability. This kind of thinking was also, in time, to find its way into Christianity in the form of Gnosticism. Arguably, a strain of this kind of anti-corporealism has endured right down to the present day.

On a different level, however, one can see in the Orphic and Stoic reflections on the mystery of evil an attempt to come to terms with the tragic dualism of human nature with its mixture of the diabolic and the divine. In short, one has here a crude pre-figuring of those themes which in Christian theology were to be accounted for by the doctrine of original sin. The mysteries and religious groupings of Greece and Rome remained a largely primitive way of life because initiation into these cults never demanded an ethical conversion: it simply held out the prospect of escape from successive returns to the world, through repeated incarnations. All the same, their expiatory 'rites' were quite revealing – the bloodless offerings and libations that had to be cast into the flames in order to placate the Furies were believed to cleanse the earth. The blood of a slain animal poured over the hands of the 'criminal' sought to externalize the internal 'stain' and thus to cleanse it. There was here a real foreshadowing of the kind of imagery which was to emerge in Christian theology, yet the full implications of this symbolism were never really developed in the Greek or Roman minds.

In the end it appears that Greece and Rome were 'no fit terrain for the development or sharpening of a consciousness of sin; there were too many obstacles to it in the shape of rationalism, intellectualism, and aestheticism. These civilizations believed human beings to be so rational and reasonable, so enthusiastic for the beautiful and the good that they could not think of them as sinners in any real ethical sense'.[26] The true authors of evil could therefore only be the gods or blind fate, thereby leaving the hapless human beings as the innocent victims of 'divine caprice or malicious destiny'.

That said, there are the beginnings of three distinct formulations of sin very gradually emerging here. In the first, sin is presented as a physical evil to be got rid of. The second portrays it as a human failing which must be remedied. The third suggests an offence against God, which must in some way be atoned for. Perhaps it is not helpful for us to think of these notions of sin as mutually exclusive. Neither should they be simply considered successive moments along the historical continuum of an evolving theology of sin. It would seem fairer to view them as co-existing components of an as yet un-systematized understanding of human fallibility.

At the same time, from the vantage point of Christian wisdom, the human lot in the Greek schema remained a rather sorry one. If the gods were also fallible and capable of malice, reality as it was experienced by human beings was always going to be something of a vicious circle. This is why Christianity was to represent such a radically new approach. The God of the Jews and the Christians was to combine omnipotence with ethical perfection. It followed that if God was all-good and humankind was enjoined to mirror this goodness on earth, then what evil there was, was not to be found in the Godhead but in the human heart. Of course, the question of blind fate or destiny still remained, and the question of pre-moral or immoral evil continued to be a problem for Jewish and Christian thinkers, and remains so to this day. But by ascribing moral goodness to the deity the Judaeo–Christian tradition opened the way for a synthesis of religion and ethics. Obeying the will of God no longer meant simply observing ritual etiquette, it now entailed imitating moral goodness. Sin would no longer be a mere failure or mistake in ritual duties; it would in future be a rejection in some sense of the will of God.

With this enhanced notion of 'voluntary evil' the Judaeo–Christian tradition was better equipped to resolve the dilemma of the Greeks and propose a new meaning and purpose to human existence. The ethico–religious concept of sin that emerged led inevitably to a new synthetic understanding of virtue. Moral activity could no longer simply be seen as an expression of human intelligence as understood for instance by Aristotle; it was instead to become part and parcel of the believer's path to salvation.

Notes

1 See Moore, G. F., *History of Religions*, T&T Clark, Edinburgh, 1920, 175ff.; and Swete, H. B., *The Forgiveness of Sins*, Macmillan and Co., London, 1917.

2 Budge, E. A. W., *Egyptian Ideas of the Future Life,* Dover, New York, 1969, 143. (N.B. Budge tended to be more than a little speculative in his approach!)

3 See Tallquist, K., *Die Assyrische Beswörungsserie,* Maqlu Leipzig,

1895. Also Lagrange, M. J., *Études sur les Religions Sémitiques,* Lecoffre, Paris, 1903.

4 See the extensive and erudite discussion in Lyonnet, S. and Sabourin, L., *Sin, Redemption and Sacrifice,* Biblical Institute Press, Rome, 1970, 127–36.

5 LaCocque, A. 'Sin and Guilt', in Mircea Eliade (ed.), *The Encyclopedia of Religion,* Macmillan, New York/London, 1987, Vol. 13, 327.

6 Ferguson, E., *Backgrounds of Early Christianity,* Eerdmans, Michigan, 1987, 170.

7 LaCoque, *op. cit.*, 329.

8 Tomlinson. R. A., *Greek and Roman Architecture,* British Museum Press, London, 1995; see also Ferguson, *op. cit.*, 174.

9 *Bellerophon Frag.* 17(19) 4, in Snell, B. (ed.), *Tragicorum Graecorum Fragmenta*, Göttingen, 1986.

10 Ferguson, *op. cit.*, 200.

11 Nock, A. D., *Conversion,* Oxford University Press, Oxford, 1933, 80.

12 Dowden, K., *Religion and the Romans*, Classical Press, Bristol, 1992.

13 Arnold, E. V., *Roman Stoicism,* University Press, Cambridge, 1911.

14 *Ibid.*, 266

15 Sen. Dial. V.36, 2, in Clode, W., *The Morals of Seneca*, Scott, London, 1896, 40.

16 Cic Tusc. Dip. *i* 16,36, in Yonge, C., *The Academic Questions of Cicero*, Bell & Sons, London, 1907, 284–474.

17 Sen. Dial. *VI* 19,4, in Clode, *op. cit.*, 133ff.

18 Epictetus. c.3ff, in Oldfather, W. (ed.), *Epictetus*, London, and Cambridge, Mass., Loeb Classical Library, 1925.

19 Sen. Dial. 36, in Clode, *op. cit.*, 39ff.

20 Antoninus, in Semet Ipsum 9.1, edited by Schenkel, H., Leipzig, 1913.

21 Diog. L. Proem 1, in Barnes, J. (ed.), *The Complete Works of Aristotle*, Princeton, 1987.

22 This point I have explored in a more detailed way elsewhere; see Connolly, H., *The Irish Penitentials,* Four Courts Press, Dublin, 1995, 14ff.

23 Livy v. 46; Caesar, vi.16; Dionysius of Halicarnassus, Vii 70; Arrian, xxxv.i; as cited in MacCulloch, J. A., *The Religion of the Ancient Celts,* Constable Press, London, 1992.

24 For more on this, see Debarge, L., Le Syncrétisme Réligieux: Druidisme et Christianisme, *Mélanges Scientifiques et Réligieuses* 46, Mars, 1989, 5–21.

25 See Sharkey, J., *Celtic Mysteries: The Ancient Religion*, Thames and Hudson, London, 1975; also Green, M. J., *Exploring the World of the Druids*, Thames and Hudson, London, 1997.

26 Graneris, G., 'The Concept of Sin in Comparative Religion', in P. Pallazzini (ed.), *Sin, its Reality and Nature: A Historical Survey,* Scepter, Dublin, 1964, 12–27.

2

The Biblical Context: God's Unfolding Story of Love

> Whoever is without sin, let him cast the first stone. (John 8.7)

Although the Jews, like the Greeks, recognized the universality of human weakness and wrongdoing, the Old Testament Scriptures often seem at first glance to be more concerned with recording particular sins than engaging in theological reflection on the nature of sin as a religious phenomenon. Ezra, for instance, speaks of an experience of sinfulness, which is almost innate: 'From the days of our fathers to this day we have been in great guilt' (9 Ezra 7). The Book of Wisdom similarly describes how sin and death entered the world through the 'envy of Satan': 'for God created man for incorruption and made him in the image of his own eternity but through the Devil's envy death entered the world' (Wisdom 2.23–4). In the later well-known Genesis accounts the story unfolds of how, in the Garden, the Devil tempts Eve and makes her promise to give the forbidden fruit to Adam: 'The serpent beguiled me and I ate' (Genesis 3.14). But here one also detects the beginnings of a much more profound theological enquiry.

The ensuing eight chapters which chart the primeval and mythic history of humankind from the Fall to the episode of the Tower of Babel have been called the 'Great Hamartology' or theology of sin. The concern here was to chart the disastrous domino effect, which is irreversibly set in train after the first act of disobedience and transgression of the will of Yahweh. The initial rebellion brings a disorder into the relationship between God and his creation when the creatures try to become like their creator. In so doing they overstep their status as creatures and their sin puts a separation between them and God. They are therefore 'sent forth from the Garden of Eden' and the effect of sin is ultimately alienation and isolation.

And yet it is not just the relationship with Yahweh which has been disordered; life itself has now taken on a very different complexion. Chaos has entered the web of human relationships and even the relationship with the natural world has been upset. Sin no longer simply concerns the lives of our proto-parents: it begins to cast its shadow over the entire human race and all creation. The emphasis here is universal; the consequences of sin have redounded not just on Israel and the Hebrews but on all of humankind. All humanity is in fact represented by the symbolic name 'Adam'. Recriminations and rationalizations abound, but despite the best efforts the consequences of sin cannot be undone (Genesis 3.14–24). Adam is henceforth to be a tiller of the soil; he and his descendants will have to engage in a 'silent combat between man and soil' in order to win their livelihood.

Eve, in turn, is destined to suffer in bringing forth new life, and the story of Cain and of the subsequent generations down to the Tower of Babel is a litany of jealousy and envy giving rise on occasion to violence, bloodlust and even death. Individual sin enters family life, one of the most basic expressions of community, and the human race must for ever bear its hallmarks. These mythic accounts attempt thus to account for the replication and reproduction of sins from one generation to the next. The estrangement of Adam and Eve is mirrored in the life story of Cain who becomes the archetypal fugitive. Here, in what Eliade calls this 'narrative of origins', one can already discern some key elements of the underlying theological understanding of sin. A first element is the damage which sin does to the relationship between Yahweh and his people – a relationship which set Israel apart from the other nations. Human pride and rebelliousness is not simply the *hubris* of Greek tragedy bringing about the downfall of the flawed hero through the blind and capricious forces of fate; it is instead an expression of rebellion against God – the Lord who has loved his creatures into being (Numbers 14.9; Deuteronomy 28.15). Sin is a wilful breaking off of the loving dialogue through which God converses with his creation and calls it to fullness of life. This dialogue will later take the form of the covenant – the pledge of intimate love, which God calls upon his people to reciprocate. In rejecting their status as creatures, the first human beings reject truth – the truth about themselves and the truth of who they really are.

Once creaturehood has been dispensed with, it follows that the creator too must be rejected, and the remainder of the rebellion is comparatively straightforward. In time, Israel will be bold enough to fashion her own gods, and the later episode of the Golden Calf (Exodus 32) provides a vivid account of this enterprise. The idol made of precious metal is within reach, malleable and is reflective of the prevailing culture.

The episode also highlights another element, namely the communal dimension of sin. The sin of the one has now become the sin of the many. It is *peša* – a collective rebellion against God and the rejection of his love and his rule. The account of the Tower of Babel, like that of the Golden Calf, traces the progress of corruptive and corrosive self-assertion as it gradually permeates the collective will of an entire people. The story becomes a metaphor *par excellence* of delusional group aspirations toward false grandeur and totalitarian unity, built upon the foundations of human pride and greed.

The Tower was to be the one whose summit allowed it to penetrate the heavens. It was to be built from one kind of brick, with one kind of mortar for a people of one single language. In dispersing the peoples after the Babel episode, Yahweh reintroduces diversity and humankind learns to distrust facile unification and monoculturalism. The account is nevertheless the climactic evidence of the virus of overweening self-assertion which first entered the will of the proto-parents and now expresses itself in the desires and aspirations of an entire nation. By the end of the 'Great Hamartology' primeval human history has come to a rather sorry pass. The human race has failed miserably to find the fullness of life, which once beckoned in Eden in the form of communion with God and community with others. It is guilty of *hattah*, of 'missing the mark', and of straying from the path of justice which Yahweh had set before it. It has instead chosen the path of power and defiance and has thus allowed itself to be led astray.

A third element emerging from these early Scriptures and their reflections on sin is the underlying conviction that, despite the trials and even the tragedy of human weakness and malice, sin does not have the last word. To be sure, Yahweh punishes his creatures for their foolishness. Adam and Eve are indeed sent forth from Eden, Cain is banished to the land of Nod, the Great Flood punishes a sinful world, and the Tower of Babel is razed to the ground. But there remains a constant concern on the part of Yahweh for his human creatures. So, despite sinfulness all around, Noah still finds favour with God, and even the destruction and dispersal of Babel gives way to the joy of the call of Israel. There is an abiding sense here that despite the chaos and corruption of sin, Yahweh still has a plan for his creation – a plan that will bring it to a new and glorious day. That plan was eventually to find its definitive expression in the covenant between God and Israel. This divine pledge of love represented Yahweh's 'election' of his people, his ultimate invitation to human beings to enter into communion with him. It was a call to Israel to reverse the forces of rebellion and rejection by freely choosing as their God the one who had freely offered them his love.

Of course, Israel was still sinful, her people were still susceptible to the vicious circle of guilt and suffering, the very clothes of Adam and Eve were a reminder of their shame, the mark of Cain accused him of his *āwôn*, his iniquity and guilt. But alienation is not definitive, the sinner may yet return to God; there is always the possibility of *shub* – a change of direction and a return to God.

As salvation history unfolds, so too does the tension between, on the one hand, humankind's attraction to the good – the *Yêtzér ha-tob* – and on the other the inclination toward evil or *Yêtzér ha-ra*. There is awareness that, even with the best intentions, humanity will fall and fail, and so the idea of atonement must be gradually developed. A priestly class is established and very specific sacrificial rites evolve that will bring about atonement for the evil committed. The book of Leviticus records the emergence of a belief that the sins of the men and women may somehow be transferred on to an animal for sacrifice. The sinful deeds of an entire community may be projected on to a blameless goat and the animal will rid them of their sin as it wanders off into the wilderness:

> Aaron shall lay both his hands upon the head of the live goat and confess over him all the iniquities of the people of Israel and their transgressions. He shall put them upon the head of the goat and send him away into the wilderness . . . The goat shall bear all the iniquities upon him to a solitary land, and he shall let the goat go in the wilderness. (Leviticus 16.21–2)

Not every account of sin in the Old Testament, however, is presented as a violation of the moral order. As was the case in the Egyptian and Babylonian civilizations, sin also included the whole area of ritual or cultic impurity. It could be a purely material transgression of the rites and ceremonies of the Mosaic Law, on the one hand, or a voluntary violation of a divine precept on the other. To the Hebrew mind, external ceremonies were a necessary complement to interior religious motivation. They were also an important element in reinforcing the bonds of community and the Israelite sense of identity over against the cult and splendid liturgies of the pagan peoples. The Mosaic Law therefore organized Jewish religious life in a profound way and placed the Tabernacle at the centre of that life. Laws of holiness extended forth from this hub to the high priests, the priests, the Levites and the people to various aspects of daily life.

Significantly, no real distinction was made between moral and ceremonial law. The Law was seen as the revelation of Yahweh to Moses and it was to be obeyed in its entirety: 'Keep my commandments and do them, I am the Lord. Profane not my holy name, that I may be sanctified in the midst of the children of Israel. I am the Lord who sanctifies you' (Leviticus 22.21–32).

This idea that the Law was divinely promulgated may well have served to reinforce the sense of intimacy which existed between Yahweh and his people. It reminded them no doubt of the pact they made with him and which had been accepted and ratified at Sinai (Exodus 19.8; 24.3). Deuteronomy and Leviticus go to great lengths to describe the sanctions and punishments which are to be the lot of those who are transgressors of the Law and, by contrast, the rewards which are to be lavished upon those who keep it.

But ritual behaviour and ritual sin are not to be understood solely in terms of obedience and disobedience. Given that external rites and ceremonies were considered to be expressive of the inner religious attitude, there had to be a harmony between the inner disposition and the outward act. In other words there was always an insistence on 'interior holiness' as well as on the holiness of the ritual. In the book of Isaiah there is to be found an expression of Yahweh's disgust at the sacrifices, which are not expressive of a true inner conversion:

> What to me is the multitude of your sacrifices? . . . I have had enough of burnt offerings of rams and the fat of fed beasts . . . Bring no more vain offerings, incense is an abomination to me . . . I cannot endure iniquity and solemn assembly. (Isaiah 1.10–18)

The Psalmist, on the other hand, reminds his listeners of the demands of true holiness: 'The sacrifice acceptable to God is a broken spirit, a broken and contrite heart O God thou wilt not despise' (Psalm 51.17). Although Yahweh wishes that everything be done in accordance with the Law, a narrow legalism will not do. He has nothing but contempt for those sacrifices which are born out of hypocrisy.

The presence of the Tabernacle, the sanctuary in the midst of the people, is also a sign that they are to be holy. If, though, by their duplicity they show themselves to be unholy, then Yahweh has no further use for them. Sacrificial rites can never become a substitute for true holiness. If performed for their own sake without reference to the inner disposition, these liturgies become shallow, hollow and ultimately sinful. Instead of sacrificial victims, Yahweh wants obedience of the heart; instead of acts of sacrifice he desires regard for God and for neighbour. In place of mere external cleanliness he requires innocent hands and a pure heart. The rites of the Mosaic Law are undeniably a means to holiness, but they do presuppose adherence to the entirety of the religious and moral law. 'Rites devoid of any ethical element would be an absurdity in the Old Testament'.[1]

The prophetic literature also goes to some lengths to graphically describe the alienating effects of sin: '. . . your iniquities have made a separation between you and your God, and your sins have hid his face from you so that he does not hear' (Isaiah 59.2). And yet the remedy is also available: 'Then you shall cry and the Lord will answer, you shall cry and he shall say here I am' (Isaiah 58.9).

For the prophets, the essence of sin, whether ritual or moral, is the deliberate rupture of personal relations between man and God. Likewise, the return to Yahweh can only be a conversion of the whole heart, a complete change in the moral life of the individual, or indeed of the community, and a renewed awareness that Yahweh will, in the words of Jeremiah, 'forgive their iniquity and remember their sin no more' (Jeremiah 31.34). Yahweh never leaves the sinner without hope. To the Hebrew mind this awareness can only be born out of a sincere acknowledgement of the truth, a frank avowal of one's awareness of the unlovely spectre of sin before the blinding holiness of God. The words of the Psalmist capture the contrite mood: 'my sin is always before me' (Psalm 51.5).

The Old Testament insists, then, upon a searingly realistic view of humankind and of its fallibility. We find here a realistic anthropology, a view of mankind, which is credible. There is no pretence that men and women are anything other than creatures, creatures who are prone to all the foibles and frailties of the human condition. There is here no 'dreamy eyed angelism . . . no imaginary island of sinless isolation . . . no outraged piety in the face of sin'.[2] On the contrary, the fallibility and fickleness of the human condition is laid bare, albeit in the context of the constancy and closeness of God's love. Indeed, the assurance of this love is never far from the thoughts of the Old Testament writers, though they did not always appreciate the extent of that love. Words were somehow incapable of expressing it, and so it was to take the events of Bethlehem and Calvary to give it full expression.

The link between salvation from sin and the promised Messiah emerges in the earliest pages of the New Testament. Matthew records the angel's words: 'You shall call his name Jesus because he will save his people from their sins' (Matthew 1.21). And yet it is fair to say that New Testament thought is still very much dominated by the horizon of covenant. That covenant continues to be understood in terms of God's loving intimacy, but now it has found its most vivid expression in the gift to the world of his only-begotten son.

The earthly ministry of Jesus too is all of a piece with the Father's loving care. The Gospels are replete with examples of Christ's tenderness and compassion towards all who encounter him. This attitude is, on numerous occasions, a source of scandal to the civic and religious leaders of the day, notably the scribes and Pharisees, for whom it appeared entirely inappropriate that a rabbi should have such familiarity with publicans, women, foreigners and sinners. The world in which Jesus lived made a rather marked separation between respectability and sinfulness so that states of life such as being a Gentile or a tax-gatherer were seen as sinful in themselves. Those who mingled publicly with publicans, foreigners and females were also guilty by association.

Yet Jesus overstepped the rigid conventions of his society and disregarded many of the traditional taboos. In so doing he demonstrated his profound disagreement with the prevailing notions of sin and distanced himself significantly from the idea of ritual sin. External impurities that could be washed clean, omissions in the ritual prayers and sacrifices, eating of the proscribed foods – all of these understandings of sin were found wanting and were seen as peripheral to the true meaning of sin. We have of course already seen how the prophets had struggled against these deficient conceptions of sin, but Jewish morality at the time of Jesus still tended to measure guilt by the external material act rather than the internal disposition toward good or evil. By contrast, Jesus taught that sin, like godliness, is ultimately a quality of the inner self, for it is 'from within, out of the heart of man' (Luke 6.45) that all good and evil thoughts and deeds come.

Since sin is a failure in a relationship of love it necessarily involves the 'heart'. For Jesus, as for the prophets before him, the response to God is rooted in the heart and to sin is really to 'harden one's heart' to God's love. This is a metaphorical vocabulary that emphasizes the inwardness and interiority of the New Testament message.

For the very same reason, the Sermon on the Mount proclaims the blessedness of the 'pure in heart'. The 'heart' is where one is present to oneself and to God, it is the seat of one's decisions and dispositions. It is also the nexus where we connect to God and a window on the immanent and the transcendent. Purity of heart and singularity of the eye therefore become biblical metaphors for authenticity and sincerity.

'The eye is the lamp of the body, so if your eye is sound, your whole body will be full of light; but if your eye is not sound your whole body will be full of darkness' (Matthew 6.22ff.). Jesus' ministry among sinners is also an acknowledgement that true morality comes from the heart and is therefore a covenantal morality.

In the Sermon on the Mount (Matthew 5–7) Jesus makes clear that in his own person he is about to establish the new and eternal covenant which will be the basis of the new law. In the so-called *antitheses*, the series of 'You have heard that it was said . . . but I say to you' sayings, he insists on the preeminence of inner attitude over external ritual prescription. Certainly God's will for humankind can be applied to human actions, but it is of still greater import that it should shape our inner dispositions. Where once the Law had condemned murder, Jesus now condemns the anger, which leads to murder (Matthew 5.22). Where previously the Law had condemned adultery, Jesus now condemns the lust, which paves the path toward sexual sin (Matthew 5.29). Right intention now takes precedence over juridical rigour. True holiness and interiority are to be preferred to external lip-service which only superficially purports to honour God but at another level actually circumvents his will through legalistic chicanery. Accordingly 'purity of heart' or sincerity of purpose has pride of place in Jesus' ethical teaching. This in turn places the emphasis on human dignity as the foundation for morality. In the discussion of the Sabbath question, for instance, Jesus forcefully argues 'The Sabbath was made for man and not man for the Sabbath'. In his own ministry too he goes beyond a rigorist's interpretation of the Sabbath law in order to afford those who suffer and those who are in need an opportunity to encounter the grace and mercy and the healing and life-giving power of God in their lives.

Jesus is therefore something of a boundary-breaker. His practice of eating in the company of 'undesirables' proved contentious and controversial and was a focus of many of the complaints that were brought against him.[3] Yet for Jesus this so-called 'table fellowship' was central to ministry: 'I came not to call the righteous but sinners' (Mark 2.17). The righteous here are those who, like the elder son in the parable of the prodigal son, are too concerned with their own status and standing to appreciate their sinfulness and need of salvation. Self-absorption and excessive self-preoccupation are the sinful pitfalls for the 'righteous'. They are diametrically opposed to the call to discipleship, which, in the final analysis, is a call to love one's neighbour and to take up the cause of the 'poor, the widow and the orphan'.

The well-known parable of the Pharisee and the Publican demonstrates the point lucidly. The proud and self-satisfied 'holy man' is so infatuated with his own exemplary but purely external generosity that he loses the measure of true justice. The humble publican by contrast knows his sins and, in that acutely painful self-knowledge, he is profoundly aware of his need. God is therefore like the loving and compassionate father who seeks out his errant child, the good shepherd who searches for his lost sheep and the woman who combs the house for her lost coin. These parables of mercy are of great importance and significance because they reveal in a striking way the image of God, which Jesus sets out to reveal in its fullness. The image is one of a loving parent who reaches out in love to sinful children and welcomes them into his arms. This is ultimately an image of love and it is this love which Jesus calls his followers to imitate.

The great commandment to love becomes the core of Jesus' ethical teaching. There are to be no limits to that love: 'Love your enemies and pray for those who persecute you that you may be children of your Father who is in heaven' (Matthew 5.44–8). For the Synoptic authors all of human failure and personal sin are to be seen in the light of the Great Commandment. This means that at one level sin is still to be seen as transgression of the divine command, but at another level there are also sins of omission, of neglect and of evil will which may not be verified in acts. One doesn't have far to go to find examples of this: the barren fig-tree occasions a rare moment of anger in the 'son of man'. The man who hid his talent is rebuked for doing nothing. The uncaring coldness of the priest and the Levite is exposed when human need stared them in the face. The goats on the king's left hand are sent to everlasting punishment for not giving the cup of water, the clothes, or perhaps the kindness which they might have given; and so too it is with Dives and Lazarus.[4]

Clearly Jesus is concerned that his disciples should live out the demands of love in all their fullness. Discipleship primarily means following him. His call is a call to live in the light of the coming kingdom just as Jesus himself did. Sin, in turn, describes failure in responding to this call, failure to live a life of true discipleship, failure to imitate the model of fraternal love which Jesus witnesses to in his life and eventually in the laying down of that life for others (Mark 10.45). True morality, true love of God is to be found in a loving regard for others. For Jesus, no ritual demand, not even worship at the altar, can take precedence over this moral claim. 'So if you are offering your gift at the altar and there remember that your brother has something against you, leave your gift at the altar and go first be reconciled with your brother and then come and offer your gift' (Matthew 5.23–4).

Sin can therefore be understood as a betrayal or at least a neglect of love. This will obviously manifest itself in negative stances and attitudes towards others and will be seen especially in the insensitivity, selfishness, vengefulness and coldness of the Pharisees. In the end though, these are sins against the love of God – a God who has fashioned creatures in his own image and likeness, a God who calls human beings to realize their true calling in and through the imitation of Christ. As someone once memorably put it, 'Christ finds fault that we have not enough of holiness to want it or of righteousness to hunger and thirst after it.'

All sin is therefore a sin against divine love and divine providence, which in the final analysis seeks only humanity's own good. For this reason refusal to acknowledge the power of God working in Christ is seen as the unpardonable sin, this is the blasphemy against the Holy Spirit because it is a closing off of the self to the very source of love and of life (Matthew 12.30–2). It is also a refusal to grow, to interact, to live in communion and to give of one's self. It is undeniably a refusal of God but it is also a refusal of the truth about one's self. As such it is the most radical form of revolt open to humankind. It represents the deliberate abandonment of good and the choice of evil under the influence of what St Matthew and St Paul were to call *anomīa,* that iniquity which can make its way into the heart and gnaw away there like a rust or cancer.

Viewed this way, sin eventually cuts the individual off

from God as a branch is cut from the vine. The sinner's heart is hardened so that he or she refuses to be receptive to God's love. In this way sin becomes a refusal of the Father's love (Luke 25), a refusal which is rooted in the free, self-determining choice of the sinner to reject. In the end the starkness of this choice is as striking as the difference between light and darkness, and this is the imagery taken up by John to describe sin's mysterious and pervasive presence in the world. He sees it as a dark power that can only be overcome by God himself. Unlike the Synoptic authors, John tends to speak of sin in the singular. He speaks of Christ as the one who came to take away the 'sin of the world' (John 1.29). Sin therefore is to be identified with darkness and unrighteousness. It is about opting for darkness rather than light. 'The light has come into the world and men loved darkness rather than light, because their deeds were evil' (John 3.19).

John has been described as the evangelist with the most feeling for the drama and the theological import of the gospel. He presents himself not only as the witness of Christ's life but also as the inspired exegete who explores the theological and spiritual dimensions of that life. John tends to speak therefore of sin in rather sombre tones as: 'fellowship with the darkness' (1 John 1.6) and of sinners as 'slaves to the devil' (John 8.24) and again of the evil one as 'the prince of this world' (John 12.31). In this way John examines sin in terms of its deepest significance within the human story and the unfolding drama of salvation. Satan is the evil one who is opposed to love and truth. Those who choose to remain in their sins demonstrate that they are not 'children of the light' but the 'sons of darkness' (John 12.36).

The fourth evangelist has therefore a keen and vivid sense of the universality of sin and yet at the same time he is no fatalist. There is also another piece to the jigsaw of the human. In Christ, humanity is reborn from God so that the divine seed now dwells within mortal flesh. 'No one born of

God commits sin, for God's nature abides in him and he cannot sin because he is born of God' (1 John 3.9). And this divine seed is the Word of God, which gives victory over the Evil One. Accordingly, the Lamb of God 'who takes away the sin of the world' is juxtaposed to the forces of darkness. These forces come from the Evil One who from the outset was for John the 'slayer, the deceiver and the father of lies' (John 8.44). Within this theatre of battle between cosmic forces the followers of Christ have to try to live out lives of discipleship. This can only be done when they each accept his own self-revelation. 'I am the light of the world. Whoever follows me will not walk in darkness; but will have the light of life' (John 8.12; cf. 1 John 1.5–7). And yet in spite of this self-revelation humankind has a constant struggle to perceive things clearly. 'The light will be among you only a little while. Walk while you have the light, so that darkness may not overcome you' (John 12.35). This struggle, this pilgrimage from darkness to light, is vividly captured in three particular episodes: the encounters with Nicodemus (John 9.1–41), the Samaritan woman (John 4.7–42) and the man born blind (John 9.1–41). Nicodemus first comes to Jesus under cover of darkness but has the courage to 'emerge into the light' and to come to Jesus' defence (John 7.50–1). The Samaritan woman is initially incredulous but through her encounter with Jesus eventually becomes a missionary to the Gentiles. The blind man, having had the courage and the faith to ask for Jesus' assistance, is rescued not only from a world of physical sightlessness but also from spiritual darkness. Because he never disputes his lowly and sinful status, he comes to faith in Jesus, but the 'established leaders' who deny their sinfulness prove themselves to be utterly blind to the truth before them.[5] For John, sin comes down in the end to a fundamental choice between on the one hand he who is 'light and love' and on the other he who is the 'Prince of Darkness'.

Like John, Paul often describes sin in terms of a power or

outside force which is opposed to God. Just as there is solidarity of all Christians in Christ, so too there is a kind of solidarity in sin, which is almost a part of the human condition. 'All have sinned and fallen short of the glory of God' (Romans 3.23). This hostile power introduced through the sin of Adam is within the human person and has entered the very flesh like a kind of occult personality. 'For I do not do the good I want, but the evil I do not want is what I do' (Romans 7.19). In this manner sin introduces a division within the very self, a fragmentation of the moral person. For Paul, sin also has a corporate dimension. He explains: 'None of us lives to himself and none of us dies to himself' (Romans 14.7). All are members of the Body of Christ, and so when one sins one not only wounds the vertical relationship with God, but one also does injury to the horizontal relationship with the Body of Christ which is the Church. So for Paul it would be difficult to overstate the seriousness of sin. According to his doctrine it takes possession of the self, alienates from God, instils hostility in the soul and leaves the individual completely rudderless and helpless. Indeed, for Paul, sin also provokes the wrath of God, but this is not so much a vindictive fury as a manifestation of divine justice. After all 'he gives us up' to whatever we prefer. Punishment therefore is but the inevitable consequence of wrongdoing in a moral universe where whatever one sows so also shall one reap.[6]

Paul sees important connections too between sin and the Law on the one hand, and alienation and death on the other. Faced with the corruption of human nature and the moral disintegration of his people, God, according to Paul, chose to intervene with a saving plan. This he achieved through the gift of the Law which was entrusted to his people, but the 'adversary' turned this to his own advantage, and the Law which was meant to forbid and to control sin actually provoked further sin because of the 'fatal fascination of the forbidden thing'.[7] In a paradoxical way the Law somehow gives rise to more sin and the tactics of the serpent in the Garden are again adopted.

All the same, sin does not have the last word and so for the disciple who has put on the new clothing of Christ there is always hope: 'For the law of the Spirit of Life in Christ Jesus has set us free from the law of sin and death' (Romans 8.2). It may be true that the old law was made not for the just but for the iniquitous, but those who follow Christ are to 'throw off' the old and 'put on' the new. They are to pass from the law of sin and death to the new law of the Spirit of life. So life in Christ frees his followers from slavery to the Law and gives them the grace through the outpouring of the Holy Spirit to live as 'servants of justice'. For Paul, the life and saving death of Jesus has brought about a paradigmatic shift from a religion of the law to a religion of love. The implications for a theology of sin are great even if it might be argued that Christians are to this day still struggling to realize that vision and to cast off the old religion of law in favour of the new religion of love. Consequently, the tension between law and love is still very much in evidence almost two millennia later.

Paul also sees sin as inescapably related to death. For him, it has a life-sapping power and it kills morally, spiritually and even physically. In Romans he explains 'The wages of sin is death' (Romans 6.23). Death, in other words, is the price of sin. It is the alienation of the soul from God, the corruption of the entire being and the severance from the source of all life. Sin brings about the disintegration of the individual and disassembles the Body of Christ. On the other hand, '. . . if anyone be in Christ there is a new Creation'. So the power of the indwelling Spirit has victory even over death.

Sometimes Paul is described as the 'apostle of faith'. To this we can add that he was also the 'apostle of love'. His great hymn to love (1 Corinthians 13) shows how *agape* or self-giving love gives new direction, new life and a renewed integration to all life's plans and energies. Where once sin had caused the sinner to fall short and to miss the mark, love now impels the disciple forward toward the new mark which is the authentic imitation of Christ. As one commentator puts it: 'In the deepest sense the Christian character is for Paul autonomous and free, neither subservient to the world nor dependent on the world but on the natural visible outflow of life with Christ.'[8]

So divine grace and the response of love, which it evokes in humankind, are the antidote to sin. 'Where sin abounds grace still further abounds' (Romans 5.20). Indeed, one has to say that throughout the New Testament sin is always viewed in the perspective of charity. Fraternal love, *agape*, or charity is considered to be the surest defence against sinful behaviour. A key index of this agapeic love is one's readiness to forgive and be reconciled. The model *par excellence* of such forgiveness and reconciliation is of course Christ himself, whose life and saving death is all about forgiveness: 'This is my blood poured out for the forgiveness of sins' (Matthew 26.28). In and through the life and death of Christ God offers unconditional forgiveness to all who believe. Jesus is therefore both the 'perfect high priest' and the blameless sacrifice, 'the Lamb of God who takes away the sins of the world' (John 1. 29). The life and death of Jesus exposes the inadequacies of the atoning structures of the Old Testament. The 'scape-goating' mechanisms have been critiqued and found wanting. Although Yahweh did not leave the Hebrew sinner without hope, the Gospels are truly 'good news' of a whole different order. Now God himself has come to visit his people, to call them to conversion and to rescue them from their sins.

The cross of Christ is therefore the primordial sacrament of redemption since it effectively demonstrates and communicates the salvific love of God. The Passion becomes the perfect assurance of God's forgiveness because it manifests the unconditional nature of divine love. The fact then that human beings err and stray and 'miss the mark', the fact that they become selfish, self-centred and self-absorbed does not influence at all the way in which God loves them. 'God shows his love for us in that while we were yet sinners Christ died for us' (Romans 5.8). Like all sacraments though, the cross is both a gift and a task. The loving pardon of God calls his creatures to mutual forgiveness, so that whoever does not forgive from the heart remains closed to the experience of God's loving forgiveness. As Christ has forgiven, so must his disciples forgive, and therefore their prayer must be: 'Forgive us our debts as we also have forgiven our debtors' (Matthew 6.12; Luke 11.4).

Thus the Church is born as a community of believers who know their weakness and their fallibility. The Holy Spirit that dwells within it is a spirit of love and forgiveness. The forgiveness of sins therefore becomes a hallmark of the early Church.

Notes

1 Mariani, B., 'Ritual Sin in the Old Testament', in P. Pallazzini (ed.), *Sin, its Reality and Nature: A Historical Survey,* Scepter, Dublin, 1964, 52.
2 Power, J., 'The Call to Penance in the Old Testament', in D. O'Callaghan (ed.), *Sin and Repentance*, Gill and Son, Dublin, 1967, 16.
3 See the extensive discussion of this in Dunn, J., *Jesus' Call to Discipleship,* University Press, Cambridge, 1992, 72–6.
4 See White, R. E. O., *The Changing Continuity of Christian Ethics*, Paternoster Press, Exeter, 1979, 105.
5 Witherup, R. D., *Conversion in the New Testament*, Michael Glazier Press, NY, 1994, 86.
6 White, *op. cit.*, 142.
7 Barclay, W., *The Mind of St Paul*, Collins, London, 1958, 140.
8 White, *op. cit.*, 102

3

The Development of the Vocabulary and the Theology of Sin

Inconstancy unnaturally hath begott
A constant habit; that when I would not
I change in vowes, and in devotione.
As humerous is my contritione
As my prophane love, and as soone forgott.
(John Donne, Holy Sonnet 19)

The kind of society we find reflected in the Acts of the Apostles and the early patristic writers belongs to the era of the primitive Christian community. It is the time of *maranatha*, of Christians who lived in a close unity of spirit with one another and whose chief thoughts were on the Lord's imminent return. For them the day of judgement was by no means a distant prospect and so the sayings of Jesus, even the difficult ones which called for mutual love, forgiveness and renunciation of wealth and common ownership of possessions, were taken with the utmost gravity. Indeed, mutual love was soon to be the hallmark of these communities. 'See how they love one another' the pagans are said to have remarked of them. Evidently there was a fraternal solidarity here of which the substantial bond was Christ himself. This bond was strengthened in time in the face of persecution and bloodshed. But fraternal love also demanded fraternal correction and reproof, and the youthful Christian Church, although active, strong and vigorous, was, nevertheless, according to her own self-understanding, still very much a Church of sinners.

Among the earliest writings of the primitive Church, one of the most celebrated was discovered as recently as 1873. Of unknown authorship, it became known as the *Didache* or 'Instructions of the Apostles'. The first six chapters of this very brief document are arguably the very first code of Christian morality; they represent a compendium or catechism of the moral teaching of the time and give us a detailed list of the various sins that are to be avoided. Among categories of sin to be found here are homicide, impurity, avarice and lying. Christians are enjoined to shun these sins of the pagans and to live out a good and worthy life, praying three times daily, fasting twice weekly, showing hospitality and forgiveness, and being attentive to their family responsibilities as well as confessing their sins before approaching the altar. 'In church you shall confess your sins . . . Before you celebrate the Eucharist confess your sins that your sacrifice may be pure'.[1] The *Didache* also makes an important distinction between sins in thought (*cordis*) and external or material sins (*operis*). The choice for Christians is ultimately a stark one: either they choose the path of the just which leads to life or they follow the way of sin that brings only death.

Shortly after the time of the *Didache* the Shepherd of Hermas took up this allegory of the two ways or choices and elaborated on the kinds of sin which can 'snare the follower of Christ'. His list is quite comprehensive and shows some rudimentary attempts at classification.

> Abstain then from evil, . . . from adultery, from drunkenness, from injustice, from many delights and pleasures, from banquetings, from excessive riches, from vain arrogance, and from an evil conscience, from overweening wisdom, and the flatteries of pride, from

> lying and detraction from hypocrisy and from every form of malice, and from all blasphemy, . . . from stealing, from deceit, from bearing false witness, from coveting the property of others from the love of evil things and from misleading men, so that they be not vain nor proud.[2]

Even so, according to the same author, all sins may be remitted provided that penance is conscientiously carried out. Hermas also delves on occasion into questions of marital morality and more particularly into the pastoral problems surrounding adultery. His intent here though is to emphasize the efficacy of penance rather than to explore at any length the nature of the sin. According to him, penance allows the sinners to take their places again like individual stones or bricks in the building of a church. All the same, the follower of Christ may only have recourse to repentance once in their lifetime and after this there ought to be no further relapse into sin.

In time a penitential system developed, affording forgiveness of sins via a once-off exclusion from the altar and an imposition of penance, as well as re-admission to the Eucharist upon its completion. As this disciplinary system of the Church began to develop, so too did the first steps toward a 'special' or applied moral theology. This development is to be observed in the writings of some of the early apostolic fathers, notably Clement of Rome and Ignatius of Antioch, but it attained a much fuller expression in the Greek apologists. These 'Fathers of the Church' sought to defend Christianity against the accusations and objections of the learned rhetoricians and philosophers who had increasingly begun to take notice of the fledgling faith community. Some of the preoccupations of the apologists are the perennial hot topics of Christian morality such as suicide (Justin Martyr), abortion (Athenagoras), religious freedom (Irenaeus), and injustice (Lactantius). Yet the apologists were also men of their time and so many of the sins, which preoccupied them, are reflective of the era in which they lived. Theophilus for instance was anxious to point out the illegitimacy of participating in gladiator games and other pagan spectacles. Hippolytus went a step further and listed those who are to renounce their professions if they ever wish to become Christian. These included civil servants, games officials, pagan statue-makers, gladiators and prostitutes. Tertullian, something of a polemicist and certainly a rigorist in matters of morality, took up the debate and added sculptors, builders of pagan temples, pagan feast organizers, bankers, incense vendors, teachers in pagan schools, soldiers and even those involved in the theatre, to the list.

Neither did women entirely escape his caustic pen; they were enjoined to wear a veil, to do penance for the 'sin of Eve' and to take care not to arouse the sexual passion of men! They were to renounce any desire to please their men-folk as this was seen as execrable. On no account were they to dye their hair as this was only an expression of ruinous pride and vanity! Although some of these examples may seem more than a little out of place to the modern eye, it must be said that the early Christians saw their refusal to conform to pagan habits as dictated not so much by a 'hatred of humanity', as Tacitus and others alleged, but by an 'exalted view of the dignity of every human life'.[3] What is more, these early and sometimes maladroit attempts at the specification of sin should not be allowed to overshadow the very real theological grappling with the underlying mystery that is also taking place in the writings of the fathers.

Reflecting on God's admonition of Cain after the murder of Abel for instance, Theophilus notes 'it is clear from them that fault resides not in the act itself, but in man, the transgressor of the Divine commandment'.[4] Athanasius develops this thought and suggests that the Fall was perhaps prompted by selfishness: 'Once human beings diverted their attention from heavenly concerns, they began to devote attention to themselves . . . with the result that at that moment they fell into bodily yearning and, to their shame, realised their nakedness'.[5]

For Athanasius the fall into self-absorption is a fall into nothingness. It is a turning away from God who is the source of all being toward the non-being out of which we are created. The idols in turn are but symbols of nothingness since they in themselves do not exist.

This mentality may seem somewhat strange today for we tend to unconsciously think of sin as the free and deliberate transgression of a divine command. Such also was the understanding of the Fathers and was described as *anomía* but alongside this there was too an insistence on the intimate link between being and knowledge. Besides, like Aristotle and others from among the voices of classical Greece and Rome, they saw a direct connection between evil (*kakía*) and ignorance (*agnōsía*). Indeed Gregory of Nissa goes so far as to define evil simply as the lack of being.[6]

One also notes on occasion in some of the Greek Fathers the term *bórboros* borrowed from profane literature.[7] The sinner was compared to someone who fell into a cesspool of falsehood, deception and iniquity. Having a great sense of the natural order and harmony of all things the Greeks tended to perceive evil in terms of what soils, tarnishes and upsets our better intentions. This disturbance of the natural order had been, as we have seen, already the subject of much reflection in the great classical tragedies where it was seen as a force transcending human relations. In a certain sense the entire cosmos was thought to somehow react against the transgression of the sinner (even, as in the case of Oedipus, where the transgressor was completely unaware of the import of his actions). In a similar way the Greek Fathers attributed 'plagues in the cities and in the nations, periods of drought and barrenness, destruction of property, earthquakes, floods, shipwrecks and the defeat of armies' to sin.[8] This cosmic understanding of sin was much broader and all-encompassing than the notion of social sin which is sometimes spoken of today. Since man was in some sense a little cosmos or microcosm (Maximus Confessor) sin would manifest itself in human terms as a disturbance in the heart, thereby setting up a division within the very self.

Although the Fathers understood humankind to be made in the image of God, sin was believed to have the effect of obscuring and darkening that image. The effect of sin, therefore, was to disrupt *theōría* – the contemplation and knowledge of God. As a result, all these aforementioned 'disharmonies' – be they cosmic, social or anthropological – were in the end only a reflection of the primary disorder which wounded the *parrēsía*, the relationship between human beings and God.[9] To be sure, sin was perceived externally but the roots were internal; they were to be found within the *logismoí*, or evil thoughts. The ultimate and decisive cause of evil was therefore our own free choice (*proaíresis*).

Chrysostom sees this as an incontestable truth, which no one can legitimately dispute.[10] For him, sins such as injustice, immodesty, lack of wisdom, hatred, envy and deception emerge in the human heart. All of these sins contaminate the created soul, which is the image of its creator, and they sully its beauty and nobility. The fact, though, that these sins emerge in the human heart need not altogether rule out the idea that there might be some kind of external 'inspiration' of the sinful idea. After all, if humankind is made in the image and likeness of a God who is all-good, where does evil come from? The only possibility open to the Fathers here was to put forward a vague explanation such as 'a thought from without', or 'provoked by demons'.

In this context it is worth noting also the influence of

Jewish ethics on some of the Fathers and in particular of the notion of the *yêsér* to which we have earlier alluded. In the Greek text this was translated as *diaboúlion*. In the *Life of Saint Anthony* demons tormented and persecuted the Anchorites in and through their own thoughts. Evagrius in turn saw demons as the 'thoughts' or 'spirits' associated with a particular vice. Consequently, an important weapon in the Christian's spiritual warfare was the practice of 'manifestation of thoughts' to a wise and worthy mentor or spiritual director.

In order to assist this practice Evagrius drew up a list of eight generic malevolent thoughts which he maintained were at the root of every sin. This list, found in the sixth chapter of his *Praktikós*, was to become in due course a classic text of Eastern Christianity. He explained that 'there are eight generic thoughts: the first being gluttony, then fornication, the third avarice, the fourth sadness, the fifth anger, the sixth sloth, the seventh vainglory and the eighth pride'.[11]

One can immediately see a similarity here with the Western idea of the seven vices. In fact these were but a version of Evagrius' own list which was later to be taken up by Gregory the Great. He inverted the order of numeration, taking a cue from the tenth chapter of Sirach which advised 'pride is the beginning of all sin' (Sir. 10.15). He also reduced the number of vices by combining vainglory and pride. In the Latin list sadness was also replaced by envy which was seen as a kind of destructive sorrow induced by the goods of others. The ultimate inspiration for Evagrius' list may well be linked to the three temptations of Jesus, onto which others would in time have been grafted drawing on concrete experience. Noting that Jesus responded to each of the Devil's temptations with an admonition from Sacred Scripture, Evagrius set out in a separate work (the *Antirrētikos*) to provide a compendium of scriptural passages which would equip the follower of Christ to combat temptations of every kind. This text was in turn divided into eight parts according to the eight generic vices, and the schema has become a regular feature of subsequent classifications of sin.

By way of theological justification for this schema, Evagrius recalled Origen's reflections on the Old Testament account of the conquest of Canaan. This episode had involved battles against seven nations each of which were opposed to the people of Israel from the time of the Exodus from Egypt onward. Egypt itself, the first nation, was seen as representing gluttony, the second lust, the third envy and so forth.

The Patristic literature therefore gradually succeeded in developing a distinct theology of sin as well as a skeletal taxonomy of vices and extensive inventory of sins. This was to be amplified and extended over the course of time according to the reflections and practical experience of the various authors. Cyprian, for instance, gave some time to the questions of theft and damage to property, as well as the issues of usury, injustice and fraud. Origen, on the other hand, took as a frame of reference the sins enumerated by St Paul in 1 Corinthians 5–11 and 6, 9–10, such as fornication, greed, idolatry and drunkenness, and adjudged these to automatically exclude the sinner from the kingdom of God. Caesarius of Arles spoke of 'capital sins' which cried out for public penitence, and his list included sacrilege, homicide, adultery, false witness, theft, pride, envy, avarice, anger, intoxication and calumny.[12]

Perhaps the Patristic author who most wrestled with the problem of sin both theologically and spiritually was Augustine. He often seemed to speak from bitter experience, and indeed his very life was often a long and tortuous battle with sin, which led only slowly and painfully to holiness. He bequeathed two classic definitions of sin to the Church. The first, to be found in the 22nd book of the *Contra Faustum*, defined sin as 'anything said done or desired contrary to the eternal law', where the eternal law is seen as an expression of

Divine Reason. The second definition, which comes from the second chapter of his *De Libero Arbitrio*, described sin classically as 'a turning away from God and a turning toward the creature'. This was more often rendered in the familiar Latin phrase '*aversio a Dio, conversio ad creaturam*'. But Augustine also had the opportunity to explain sin in much more concrete terms in his sermons. Here he reminded his listeners that:

> all sin is covetousness for the sinner arrogates to himself the good that is God's. All sin is fornication, for instead of rejoicing chastely in God, the sinner enjoys created things lustfully, all sin is idolatry, for the sinner, instead of serving God, becomes the slave of a multitude of idols. And since God is light, sin brings with it darkness; since God is the life of the soul, sin is its death.[13]

Echoing earlier Johannine and Pauline concerns, Augustine argued that there was a dualism at work in the human condition which was the dualism of darkness and light, flesh and spirit, sin and grace. Humanity had to struggle therefore with the dialectic of sin throughout four stages of its history. The first of these was the era 'before the law', which was the era of the Fall. This was a time of darkness and confusion brought about through sinful disobedience. The second period was the time 'under the law', the era of the Covenant where new strength was given to God's people even though the law for some (as Paul observed) became only a new form of slavery. The third era was the time 'under grace', the age of the Church to which Christ had given his saving grace. In Christ all sins, just as death itself, would be overcome and here Augustine distinguished between three degrees of sin. Taking an analogy from the miraculous episodes in the Gospels he points to the three people whom Christ raised from the dead and shows how each is representative of one of these degrees. Jairus' daughter, who had only just died before Jesus arrival at their home, symbolized hidden and undetected sin. The son of the widow of Nain, who had lain for a whole day, represented sin in deed or act. Finally Lazarus, over whom the stone of the tomb had been definitively closed, represented those who were buried in habitual sin. But Christ had the power to free them from the chains of bondage and death, and in him too all humanity is just as surely freed from their sins.

The fourth and final era was the time 'of peace'. It was the time which was promised to the followers of Christ and which they yearned for unceasingly: 'You have made us for yourself O, lord and our hearts are restless 'til they rest in you.'[14]

The 'inspiration' of sin therefore, according to Augustine, was not so much demonic as based in human desire. He identified three sources of sin: pride, curiosity and carnal desire. To these three causes, he believed, all other sins could be traced. All these other sins could also be graded according to their gravity. Unlike the Stoics, who had taught that all sins were equal, Augustine saw it as a self-evident truth that *peccadillos* could not be equated with serious sin. In a rare moment of humour he argued: 'if these two things are the same, just because they are both faults, then rats and elephants are the same because they are both animals, and so are flies and eagles because they both fly!'[15] This led Augustine to make a distinction between sin *ad mortem* that broke the bond of communion, and sins which were more pardonable. Such errors were to be regarded as *veniabiliora.*[16] This division laid the foundation for the classic distinction between mortal sin on the one hand and venial sin on the other, and it largely remained so ever since, even though it was to be taken up later and developed into a coherent system by the scholastics. It is therefore not without reason that scholars came to call Augustine the 'incomparable master' of the theology of sin. His keen sense of sin, scientific approach and penetrating insight into the human condition as well as his implacable faith in the ability of the Risen Christ to answer humankind's deepest yearnings are all very evident in his comprehensive treatment of the subject.

Alongside this formal theological enquiry, the penitential practice of the primitive Church throughout the time of the Fathers continued to follow the formula outlined by St Paul in 1 Corinthians 5.5 and 2 Corinthians 2.10. The sinner was first excommunicated or 'bound' and later reconciled to the community or 'loosed' through public penitence. Public penance was often carried out during Lent, beginning with confession of sins before the bishop and the community on Ash Wednesday. The penitents had then to undertake the public penance throughout Lent, and like the catechumens they had to leave the Sunday eucharistic celebration before the consecration. Penitents were often enjoined to cover themselves in ashes to recall Adam and Eve's expulsion from the Garden of Eden. Reconciliation was then completed on Holy Thursday.

Perhaps because of the rather severe nature of Public Penance a new form of penance began to emerge in the Celtic lands, especially Ireland, in or around the sixth century. This new penitential practice was private and reiterable and although very harsh by today's standards was very much less taxing than what had gone before. What is more, because priests rather than bishops administered the new system, a need gradually emerged for handbooks, which would offer some guidance to the confessor. As a result a new literary genre came to birth in the form of the 'penitential'. This was intended as a manual for use by all priests engaged in the 'cure of souls'. The earliest of these written in Irish monasteries and in their daughter houses on the European mainland in the sixth, seventh, and eighth centuries provide fascinating insights into the understanding of sin which were operative at that time in the Celtic Church. They also give detailed reference to the kinds of sin that might be confessed. Often arranged under John Cassian's 'octade' of vices or capital sins, which had come to them via the writings of Caesarius of Arles, saintly authors of the penitentials were never squeamish about penning references to even the most explicit accounts of violence or human sexual behaviour. For this reason they have perhaps been somewhat neglected throughout the course of theological history. Nineteenth-century compilations of the texts sometimes carried a ghoulish figure on the cover together with a skull and crossbones and a foreboding whip, but even these were a progression from former eras of learning which sought to suppress the texts for what was considered to be their pornographic content. One respected historian lamented:

> The penitential literature is in truth a deplorable feature of the medieval church. Evil deeds, the imagination of which may perhaps have dimly floated through our minds in the darkest moments are here tabulated and reduced to system. It is hard to see how anyone could busy himself with this literature and not be the worse for it.[17]

Certainly these manuals were for the most part poorly written and wretchedly copied and from a literary standpoint among the rags and tatters of Church Latin literature. At another level, though, they are important documents from historical, sociological and theological points of view. The texts covered an enormous range of sins and of human misbehaviour. Even a cursory glance at the Penitential of Columbanus for instance reveals a wide spectrum of wrongdoing, including theft, drunkenness, violent acts, homicide, dishonesty, perjury, lust, fornication, adultery, masturbation, homosexual acts, bestiality, magic-making, pagan worship, as well as breaches of monastic and liturgical discipline. Penances often involved very severe fasting and sometimes corporal punishment. This was consistent with the prevailing monastic spirituality where great value was laid on heroic acts of mortification such as reciting the Psalms while standing in icy waters, or standing for long periods in prayer with the arms cruciform – a practice known as the *crosfhigil* or *crucis vigilia.*

Yet in spite of the severity of the Penitential literature there is also evidence of a gentler and more humane spirit. In their practice of 'curing sin' by enjoining the requisite virtue there was an indication that the understanding of repentance was ultimately therapeutic rather than vindictive.[18] The penitentialists were also careful to distinguish between sins of thought and sins of deed. Distinctions too were made between the same fault committed by a monk or a lay person. Age, state of health, degree of learning, force of pressure, and whether or not a sin had become habitual were also taken into account as factors in determining the gravity of a sin, or at any rate in deciding upon the severity of the penance. Columbanus, for instance, in his penitential, monastic rule and sermons, laid great emphasis on the need to uncover the personal component in sinful activity. Perhaps there was some evidence here of a more profound understanding of sin than mere transgression of the law. He seemed to grapple in a very real way with the metaphysical as well as the chronological dimensions of sin. For him, as for St Paul, the basic sin was estrangement from God. In one of his celebrated sermons he explained it thus: 'Your life is a net for you, you are ensnared willing or unwilling, in yourself you have the matter of entanglement, in yourself you do not have the means of release.'[19]

Sinfulness was therefore understood as a kind of propensity to alienation or estrangement from God, which could enslave the individual. Only Christ's power could overcome this slavery and free his followers 'from the net' initially through baptism and subsequently through penitence. Columbanus explained how this eventually led to the restoration of the image of God within the penitent and was endorsed in a real change in concrete human behaviour. 'For the love of God is the restoration of his image. But he loves God who observes his commands . . . And true love is not in word only but in deed and in truth.'[20]

The severity of penances was nevertheless to prove something of an 'Achilles Heel' for the penitentials. In time it became possible to have lengthy penances 'commuted' to shorter, less severe ones and to have one's 'soul-friend' or confessor vicariously accept part of the penitential burden. While this was laudable in its intent there were fundamental weaknesses in such a policy. Subsequent experience was to show that the practice of commutations too easily fell foul of commercialism and abuse, and the nuanced language of sin easily became obscured in a commercial logic of offence, penalty and tariff. This kind of commercialism was perhaps a forerunner of the buying and selling of indulgences which became commonplace in the Middle Ages. One might say a kind of 'trading in futures' with a difference! So while private penance was here to stay, the more sophisticated accounts of sin which were certainly to be found in germ in the penitentials became rather lost in the degeneration toward tariffed penance.[21]

While the manner in which penitents repented of their sin gradually changed from the old public model to the private approach as the Irish monks established new houses throughout Europe, new systematic penitential and pastoral *summae* also evolved. These were but very distant descendants of the original penitentials but they continued to be *Summae Confessorum* that sought to respond to the needs of confessors. Very gradually a new theology was also beginning to emerge. This aimed at ever more exact definitions and a precise rule of life. Scholasticism, as it became known, sought, like the architecture of the time, to present religious thought and action in a much more systematic and rational way. The Middle Ages began to fashion *summae* not only in theology but also in stone and stained glass. It was to become the era of the great cathedrals, of the emergence of gothic architecture, and of the sharp, precisely calculated arches pointed heavenward. The cathedrals became monuments to multiplicity and order in stone while the great theological summaries fulfilled the same role in a written medium.

A new optimism was abroad and that optimism was nowhere more evident than in the theology of Thomas Aquinas (1225–74), the most important and influential thinker of the Middle Ages. His thought diverged markedly from viewpoints which saw human beings and cultures as largely sinful. For Aquinas, human nature was essentially good, and since divine grace builds upon nature, human beings were capable of true greatness. Yet Thomas did not ignore the dark side of human nature either. He considered sin to be capable of wounding but not of corrupting humanity. There was in his thought a strong point of continuity with the scriptural and traditional accounts of sin. For Aquinas, sin was a disordering power whereas grace was an ordering principle.

> From the turning of the human will away from God proceeds disorder into all the powers of the soul. So the form of the determining moment in original sin is the lack of primal order through which the will was in harmony with God; all the other disorder in psychological powers is related to this original sin like the material for sin, or like its particular moments.[22]

Aquinas believed the human inclination toward sin manifested itself 'in a psychological troika': a tendency of the practical judgement toward egoism, emotions that were too strong and a will that was either too forceful or too weak.[23, 24] In succumbing to any one of these, human beings risked mistaking illusory happiness for true happiness. Human nature was after all essentially rational. Reason therefore had to be foremost. It had to direct human life and lead human beings to ultimate happiness. Sin on the other hand betrayed reason and therefore betrayed human nature. It was the underside, so to speak, of human greatness. Because human beings are capable of choosing greatness they are also capable of choosing evil. Because they are capable of opting for fulfilment they also have the capability to choose fragmentation and disintegration.

For Thomas, sin, like all other human choices, was a step toward a particular goal and every sin found its essential character from its goal but its essence was a disregard for the rule of reason and an option for disorder or chaos. In the *Prima Secundae* questions 71–74 Thomas explored this idea at some length. There he presented sin as a kind of rebellion against the very ordering principle of creation itself and a turning toward disintegration and nothingness. Sin for St Thomas was

> a disruption of that command (of reason) . . . a dispersion of that concentrated power with a resultant state of civil war in the individual, of a scattering of his powers on goals totally unworthy of his humanity; it was a wasting of human energy, a complete failure of accomplishment, a smashing of the mirror in which was imaged the beauty and the power of God.[25]

For Aquinas, the disintegrating power of sin was pernicious because the unifying principle of reason was swept to one side and with this the cohesion of the moral life lost integrity. It became an unconnected series of merely disparate acts and of self-interested choices.

The work of the nominalists Duns Scotus (1265–1308) and Ockham (1285–1349) differed markedly from Thomas. They laid much less emphasis on the cultivation of virtue and more on the importance of the individual moral act and its concrete circumstances. An attempt to determine sinfulness by case study method or casuistry ensued. While there were very good reasons why a scientific means should be found for bridging the divide between the area of general principles and that of concrete situations, it has to be recognized that not every casuist succeeded in realizing that goal. In its worst and most degenerate expressions some casuistry became little more than a mechanism for re-defining sin for personal and ultimately selfish motives. This only served to provoke a predictable backlash in the form of a new rigorism and legalism. In hindsight, history has clearly shown that neither the extreme sophist nor legalist approaches were ever able to deal adequately with the reality of sin for they each failed to take seriously its inner dynamism which Augustine, Aquinas and many of the Patristic authors had sought to discover.

As the Christian family became more divided, the Protestant reform movements, inspired by and derived from Martin Luther (1483–1586) and John Calvin (1509–1604), among others, tended to focus on sin rather than sins. This marked change of emphasis was to find expression in the churches of the Reformed tradition. Luther's theology was, as he often claimed, basically Augustinian but its ramifications were much more radical. As a young monk the biblical picture of divine wrath against sin particularly struck Luther. Allied to this was a keen and profound sense of his own sinfulness and an awareness of the 'self-interestedness' or 'curving in upon itself' of all human flesh which for him infected even the life of faith itself. Instead of seeking the good of one's neighbour there was always the temptation to 'acquire the virtue' of neighbour love. Instead of being humble there was the desire to 'excel' at humility. Luther expresses this memorably in his description of two different kinds of sinners. There were those he believed who veered off the road to the right. They were the zealous who, like the scribes and Pharisees of Jesus' day, succumb to their own egoism. There were also those who strayed to the left. These were the 'public' sinners, the men and women of 'easy' virtue who too easily fell prey to their passions. As he saw it there was no way of avoiding these pitfalls apart from a radical change of direction, and this would prove easier for the 'conventional' sinner than for the self-righteous one. In each case the sinner was guilty of a certain idolatry which mistook an interim good for moral goodness. Therefore 'idolatry . . . consists chiefly in the state of a heart that is intent on something else and seeks health and consolation from creatures, saints or devils; that neither cares for God nor looks to him for any good, even for help.'[26]

Calvin too had a stark sense of the corruption of human nature whereby humanity, even though by nature dependent on God, nevertheless craved independence. What is more, the animosity was not only between man and God, for even within, man was divided against himself. He was forever caught between an ethic of self-love on the one hand, and an ethic of fear on the other. Sin in all its myriad expressions was then but the consequence of fear and egoism, transgression of law, warfare, and every form of man's inhumanity to man. The rebelliousness of corrupt human nature left man in a state of virtual anarchy.

> Original sin may be defined as a hereditary corruption and depravity of our nature, extending to all parts of the soul, which first makes us obnoxious to the wrath of God and then produces in us works which in Scripture are termed works of the flesh.[27]

Central then to the Reformers' notion of sin was the idea of original sin as sinful concupiscence that remained after baptism and found expression in the sins of daily existence. This could only be overcome through grace, which was seen as not so much 'building on nature' in the manner of the scholastics but as recreating an almost totally fallen human nature.

The Catholic counter-Reformation was to see the appearance of a new type of manual, the first probably that of John Azor (1603). These systematic works were planned around the training of confessors who would assist penitents in an accurate examination of conscience and the confession of mortal sins 'according to their number and species' as required by the Council of Trent. The same council had rejected Luther's doctrine on original sin, arguing instead that it didn't destroy human freedom and that its effects were wiped out by baptism. This methodology in Roman Catholic moral theology enshrined in Trent lasted by and large until midway through the twentieth century, by which time the limitations of the approach were becoming apparent. Chief among these were an unhealthy preoccupation with sin, an excessive casuistry aimed at avoiding sin or more especially escaping punishment. There was also, on occasion, a confusion of positive law with moral law, a tendency to neglect Scripture, and an over-emphasis on individual rectitude to the detriment of social awareness.

From the moment the Church began to regularize the formation of clergy and train them for the confessional, it had become imperative that pastors should also be equipped to deal with the practicalities of sin as they found expression in the concrete lives of penitents. This probably tilted the balance in the Catholic tradition away from a dynamic approach and toward a more static understanding of sin as failure before the law. Nevertheless there was also an immense pastoral engagement here which brought a new framework for the understanding of sin into the minds of clergy and people alike.

Catholic theology did itself of course have a theology of original sin, but this was not nearly so central to everyday life as was the case in the Reformed tradition. In a highly compartmentalized theological system original sin tended to be dealt with under the rubric of dogma rather than as an aspect of the moral life. Increasingly the need was being felt for a new synthetic theology of sin, which could somehow combine the earlier dynamic patristic account with the more precise and applied pastoral and ethical wisdom of the manuals. The stage was set therefore for a thoroughgoing renewal of the theology of sin and for a more contemporary language with which to present it to the modern world.

Notes

1 *Didache,* 4, in Dressler, H. *et al.* (ed.), *The Fathers of the Church* (Vol. 1), CUA Press, Washington, 1981, 167–86.

2 *Hermas Mand,* 8, *ibid.*, 225–35.

3 See Edwards, David L., *Christianity: the First Two Thousand Years,* Cassell, London, 1997, 56.

4 *Ad Autol*, in Praten, Dods and Smith, *The Writings of Tatian and Theophilus*, T&T Clark, Edinburgh, 1895, 49–108.

5 *Contra Gentes*, 3, in Migne, J. P., *Patrologiae Cursus Completus: Series Greca* (subsequently cited as PG), Paris, 1857–1866, Vol. 25–3-97.

6 *De Anima et Resurrectione*, PG 46, 93B.

7 See Aubineau, M., Le thème du 'bourbier' dans la littérature greque profane et chrétienne, *Revue des Sciences Réligieuses* 47, 1959, 185–214; also Špidlík, T. and Gargano, I., *La Spiritualità dei padri greci e orientali,* Borla, Rome, 1983, to which I am indebted for many of the insights on the Greek Fathers.

8 Basil, *Quod Deus* 5, PG 31, 337CD.

9 Maximus Confessor, *Ad Thalassium Prol.*, PG 90, 253CD.

10 PG 58, 576 C.

11 *Praktikós,* 6, in PG 40.

12 Sermon 179.2, in *Corpus Christianorum Series Latina* (subse-

quently cited as CCL), Turnhout, 1953, 104, 725.

13 *De Civ. D.*XX-VI, P4 XLI. 665, in Migne, J. P., *Patrologia Latina* (subsequently cited as PL), Paris, 1844–1864, Vol. 41.

14 *De Divers Quest* LIV, P4XL, 38, in PL 40.

15 *Letters,* CIV, PLXXXIII, 394, in PL 33.

16 Tertullian, of course, and the Montanists had already used the term *mortalia* to represent the deadly sins of idolatry, blasphemy, false-witness, fornication, murder, fraud and lying, all of which they deemed to be unforgivable.

17 See Plummer, C. (ed)., *Venerabilis Baedae Opera Historica*, 2 vols, 1892, 1896. Clarendon Press, Oxford, 1956 (reprint), clvii–clviii.

18 Pierre Payer has argued this quite successfully in 'The Humanism of the Penitentials and the Continuity of the Penitential tradition', *Medieval Studies,* 46, 1984, 340–54. I have also emphasized this point throughout my book *The Irish Penitentials and their Significance for the Sacrament of Penance Today*, Four Courts Press, Dublin, 1995.

19 Columbanus Inst. III, in Walker, G., *S. Columbani Opera*, Irish Academy, Dublin, 1957, 60–121.

20 Columbanus Inst. XI, *ibid.*

21 I have made this case at some length in *The Irish Penitentials* (*op. cit.*).

22 *Summa Theologica* I–II, 82, 3, in Aquinas, *Summa Theologiae*, Blackfriars, London, 1963, Vol. 24.

23 *Summa Theologica* I–II 82, 3, *ibid.*

24 See O'Meara's insightful commentary in O'Meara, Thomas F., *Thomas Aquinas Theologian,* University Press, Notre Dame, 1997, 117–18.

25 Farrell, W., *A Companion to the Summa*, Vol. 1, Part 2, Sheed and Ward, London, 1974 (reprint), 271.

26 Luther, *The Large Catechism*, Fortress Press, Philadelphia, 1959 and 1983.

27 Calvin, *Institutes II, I*, John Knox Press, Louisville, Kentucky, 2001.

4

Rediscovery, Renewal and Revitalization

But I don't want comfort. I want God. I want poetry. I want real danger. I want freedom, I want goodness, I want sin. (Aldous Huxley, *Brave New World*)

The deliberations of the so-called Tübingen School and its emphasis on the dynamic character of Christian morality, together with the likes of Joseph Mausback (1861–1931), Otto Schilling (1874–1956) and Fritz Tillman (1874–1953) paved the way for a marked change of focus within the theology of sin. These theologians tended to accentuate the virtues over the commandments and to insist on Christian morality as first and foremost imitation of Christ.

A fresh discovery of the Thomistic concept of charity understood as the 'form' of all virtues and a renewed attention to the personal and dialogical character of the Christian life helped moral theology to move beyond a mere 'morality of the confessional'. The impetus was toward what the Second Vatican Council was to call 'a more scientific exposition' and 'livelier contact with the mystery of Christ and the history of salvation'. This in turn led to a move away from the excessive casuistry of the manualist era and its punctilious preoccupation with observing laws. The fruits of a more systematic scripture scholarship were also to be seen. Jesus' insistence on the pre-eminence of the permanent and basic moral law over ritual prescriptions and of inner disposition over external legality was explored at great length. The so-called 'Great Commandment' of love also became more and more central to contemporary moral theology and in particular the inescapable link between love of God and love of neighbour was once more brought to the fore. Rediscovery of Jesus' interpretation of neighbourly love in an absolute and universal sense, so that its scope was now limitless, brought with it inevitable criticism of a theology of sin, which had become legalistic and minimalist. Manualist insistence on the commandments and the deductive theological method, which this implied, had led inevitably to the exhaustive listing of sins and an elaborate taxonomy of misdeeds and misbehaviour.

Renewal of moral theology in favour of a positive accentuation of discipleship and the imitation of Christ certainly reawakened interest in the virtues and vices and in the 'tendencies of the heart' which underpin human action. An attempt to understand the roots of sinful behaviour was now considered more important than precise enumeration of misdeeds and sinful actions. This approach based as it was on the 'Great Commandment', also re-focused the moralists' scrutiny on sins of omission as well as of commission. In other words, sin was no longer merely the contravention of law and the transgression of boundaries, although of course these remained sinful realities. There was here a new awareness of the sinfulness of not doing enough, of not caring enough, of not serving enough and ultimately of not loving enough.

Sin could now be understood in terms of a failure in love – a rejection of the personal call of God. It was not simply to be summed up in the infringing or breaking of norms because at root sin was something much more profound; it was nothing less than a refusal to commit oneself to the process of salvation history.

Influenced by a strong renewal of interest in personalist philosophy theologians described how the call to life, the call to discipleship, the call to love was fundamentally a call to relationship, relationship with God and with one's fellow human beings. Sin was therefore a wounding or rupturing of these key relationships or even a failure to realize their full potential. There was a new realization that, from the Judaeo–Christian point of view, the meaning, substance, and consummation of life is summed up in our love of God and love of neighbour and that the entire force of the Great Commandment insists that these two loves may not be separated.[1] It followed therefore that the path toward discovering the 'meaning, substance and consummation of life' was to be found in human relationships and in the virtues of justice, tolerance, fraternity, respect and forgiveness which sustained them. Some modern accounts of sin also began to re-examine Pauline theology – in particular the notion of *kenosis*, the self-emptying of God who took on the human condition with its attendant sufferings and limitations. Here was where Christ showed the path of true love, of self-denial and of self-emptying. Christ therefore became for humankind the new creation, the personification and incarnation of the new call to love. In future, all human actions were to find a reference in Christ, every moral failure was to be viewed in the light of the new ethical criteria – the call to love as Christ loved, even on his death on the cross. Consequently, Christian morality was also intensely personal for it took place within the framework of the I–You relationship of the disciple to Christ.

In this perspective the struggle against sin lost some of the negative character which had served to fossilize its true meaning. It was no longer simply a question of fleeing from a taboo or 'avoiding occasions of sin' as though one were gingerly stepping on eggshells. Instead, sin was now conceived as all that kept the individual from realizing, from making real that 'newness of life' (Romans 6.4) which was their fundamental calling. In other words it was a 'failure to do the good that one could do in order to develop one's own insight, ones own sensitivity, freedom and creativity. Sin is a failure or refusal to grow . . . a refusal of responsibility and co-responsibility'.[2]

If the essence of sin was to deliberately refuse to participate in the call to love and the call to make love real in the world and in one's life it followed that to act virtuously meant to comprehend the meaning of the covenantal call. It meant that one gives a personal response to God's invitation of love. All this translated in effect into a renewed understanding of moral theology, which saw morality in the context of a vocation to be lived. It was therefore the task of this theology to discover afresh the biblical context of covenant established by his only Son. By extension, this renewed vision of morality also implied growth toward a relative maturity, toward an appreciation of what one was doing, and an awareness of the importance of one's attitudes and actions.

Sin presupposed too a certain freedom and ethical awareness. It took for granted an adequate internalization of moral principles and beliefs. Without such internalization the capacity to act morally and equally to act immorally would be significantly impaired. As a result, a basic understanding of the process of human growth toward psychological maturity also became important in the new vision. The interiorization of moral responsibility presupposed the capacity 'to weigh moral values with an upright conscience and to embrace them by personal choice'. If, as psychology suggested, human conduct was in the early years regulated from without by means of taboos, controls and promises of reward or punishment, it then became paramount that at a certain point the individual would attain a sufficient level of personal maturity to enable him or her to achieve moral autonomy. Where such autonomy has not been achieved, the capacity to sin would also be significantly reduced.

There was always the danger of regression toward a

pharisaic concept of sin. Like the attitude of the mistaken elder brother in the parable of the 'prodigal son' the emphasis could be placed on obeying orders and observing law to the detriment of deepening the relationship with the Father.[3] This then was the terrain out of which the reflections on sin at the Second Vatican Council emerged.

The 'Pastoral Constitution of the Church in the Modern World' – *Gaudium et Spes* – in its treatment of the subject insists on four essential components of the Christian hamartology.[4] The first is the question of human freedom. Sin in effect is described as destructive of freedom. But that freedom is nonetheless understood to be an essential aspect of human nature. It is a transcendent quality, which allows the individual to choose, to act, and to behave precisely as a particular person. Human beings have free will. They are not simply puppets on a stage – the playthings of gods as the ancient Greeks would have had it. Certainly, concrete acts may be influenced or impeded or even determined to a greater or lesser extent, but in the final analysis this is as a result of external factors. Human freedom and free will are crucial therefore, not alone at the level of particular categorical acts but also at the fundamental level of what it means to be human. Sin entails in some respects an abdication of this freedom; a 'will to slavery' as St Paul might have put it.

The observation that revelation is borne out by experience is the document's second insight. Human experience itself suggests that sin has a disassembling, disintegrating effect on the human person. Sin diminishes the individual and prevents him or her from achieving true fulfilment. This is the essential and integral anthropology that is at the heart of the Christian worldview. In the light of revelation, sin cannot be viewed in a purely juridical way. It must be understood instead in its full anthropological, social and cosmic dimensions.

The tension and duality which is to be found in human

nature between the call of the good and the temptation to evil is the focus of the third insight. This is the essential drama of the human condition. 'All human life, whether individual or collective, shows itself to be a dramatic struggle between good and evil, between light and darkness.' And yet Christ is the answer to this tragic predicament. As Irenaeus puts it, on account of his great love he becomes what we are, that he might make us what he is. It is true that sin has deeply corroded human nature but the image of God has not been erased. Christ has overcome sin and its consequences. Through our own participation in the saving work of Christ we too engage in the struggle against sin.

This forms the basis of the document's final insight: namely that, as St Paul assures us, 'the Lord has come to free man from his chains of bondage'. On its own, humankind is incapable of attaining salvation. Despite the claims of Pelagianism it is only in and through the grace of Christ and his Holy Spirit that one can live authentically. So the Holy Spirit is truly the mainspring of the moral life. The rejection of sin no less than the life of virtue cannot be achieved 'under one's own steam' for it is the grace of the Spirit which gives the highest and final determination to our being and our activity'.[5]

What we are seeing in these conciliar reflections is a very marked turn toward the person – but the person is nonetheless understood here in a profoundly religious way. The Council is rejecting the more extreme claims of some within the 'new epistemology' and the human sciences that human freedom is irremediably compromised. It argues instead that human beings made in the image and likeness of God enjoy freedom as a gift from God. God has made us the kind of beings we are, persons endowed with intelligence and freedom – because he willed to create beings to whom he could give his own life and love. Furthermore, because all are united with Christ through grace, all have the freedom to love as he loved with a sacrificial redeeming love.

Sin is to be understood therefore as a freely chosen response that opposes itself to God and to his will for us. It is only because we can truly act freely that sin can be described as personal. The personal character of sin suggests responsibility – the ability to respond, to have interpersonal dialogue and interpersonal relationships. But sin causes a rift, a rupture in these relationships. The experience of being a person 'is radically affected by sin'.[6] Sin is therefore both personal and interpersonal. Its malice cannot be adequately summed up in the violation of an extrinsic law. The sinner and those who are wronged both experience its alienating effects. For this reason the new emphasis can be described as 'personalist' – so long as one understands this term as involving both the personal and interpersonal dimensions.

This renewed theological understanding of sin rejects the idea that sin is a straightforward synonym for wrongdoing. Instead it is an object of revelation. It describes a reality, which involves our relationship with God. Were God not to exist one could not speak meaningfully of sin in the same way. There would only be the failure to live up to the moral demands of human civilization and society. What is more, if God is only fully known as the source and summit of revelation in and through the word which is made flesh, it follows that sin is not understood in its fullness other than through knowledge of Jesus Christ. Grasping the seriousness of sin means comprehending the truth of the person of Christ. Therefore in speaking of sin one is immediately confronted with the Other, with the notion of the radical otherness which is God. Revelation itself thus shatters any selfish or individualist understanding of sin that we may have. If this is so, sin, far from being one's own business, is by definition a reality which directly concerns the other.[7] Sin is both a God-oriented and other-oriented reality. It is this truth which exposes the falseness of a 'personal checking account' understanding of sin. Precisely because we understand ourselves as made in the image and likeness of a God who is a relational being, sin, which obscures that divine image in us, manifests itself as a relational reality. It hampers and obstructs the task of every Christian, which is described in the Gospel of Matthew as love of God, love of neighbour and, in the right manner and measure, love of self.

Viewed in this light, it was abundantly clear how impoverished a theological account of sin could become if it were reduced to a mere science of the licit and illicit. While it was true that sin remained as in Augustine's classical definition 'any wilful thought, word or deed contrary to the law of God' it was equally apparent that this definition could be very easily misinterpreted along the narrow legalistic lines of man-made law. This would only serve to obscure the 'insight into the stark reality of sin as a diminution of our own being and as an offence against God who has made us and loves us as a father and friend'.[8]

On the other hand, if sin is personal, interpersonal and relational it is a dynamic reality, which cannot be adequately described by a static legalistic vocabulary. Neither is it something that can readily be brushed aside when individually or collectively we become wearied of the idea. The context of sin after all is the moral life of the individual, which is a progression, a gradual discovery, and realization of self in response to God and neighbour. That progression can therefore be hampered and even stalled by sin. This understanding of the sinful choice sees it not just as a breach of man-made law. It is also an evil or privation which runs counter to the eternal law 'which blocks the fulfilment of human persons on every level of existence, having and twisting the person in his or her depths'.[9] It also damages community and severs the communal relationship with God. Society is thereby deprived of the openness it can and ought to have to fulfil the good of human persons.

A fresh anthropological emphasis on the progressive character of human life is therefore essential. To be human is to grow and to develop. Each person is on a path to maturity. Moral ideals and virtues cannot be 'downloaded' like information onto a computer disk. Human life is more like a dynamic and dialogical pilgrim's progress through the challenges and vicissitudes of life. This dialogical quality of life involves growth through faith and failure. Human beings are gradually drawn into the mystery of God, but the path may well be one of pitfalls and potholes. The power of sin exists in all human beings but so too does the grace of the Holy Spirit which continues to transform them into the image of Jesus Christ. There is then a 'supernatural dynamism' at work within us and it is in this ethical and existential framework that we encounter sin and grace.

It became a particular emphasis of contemporary theology then that, as well as being a call to discipleship, the divine call was also a call to communion. Just as the individual believer in the Old Testament could not be thought of as being apart from the 'people of God' nor in the New Testament as being outside the 'Body of Christ', so being Christian had always involved a corporate or ecclesial dimension. It was in and through relationships with the Other and others that one realized one's personhood. The measure by which we are able to forget ourselves, or die to self, was also to be the measure by which we discover our true selves and reflect the image of Christ. Community, fellowship and fraternity were therefore evidence of the work of the Holy Spirit within the human heart. Whereas sin isolates, alienates, disassembles, disintegrates and diminishes, grace builds up, unites, binds and reconciles. As an ethical and religious outlook *personalism* does not insulate the believer from reality; on the contrary it re-focuses his or her gaze on the key relationships which are the foundation of what it means to be person. The life of discipleship therefore transcends morality by raising it into the realm of grace. Yet nothing which is naturally good should lose its value in the supernatural order. The Christian ideal is not a dismissal of the Greek ideal but is instead a completion of it. It is, as the Council had suggested, an ideal which is still susceptible of 'scientific exposition', but one that is nourished also by the fruits of Scripture. As with the Sermon on the Mount the intent of conciliar and post-conciliar theologies was not to alter 'one jot' the exigencies of the law. It was much more a summons to trawl and quarry more comprehensively the full theological import of what sin is in all its personal, societal, communal, ecological and cosmic dimensions.

There is no doubt that some viewed this whole enterprise as a somewhat retrograde step. They favoured a return to a more old-fashioned, no-nonsense conception. But experience had already shown that this could too easily lead to an exploitation of human beings by abusing their experience of guilt and culpability. Even a cursory glance at history would clearly demonstrate that there is some truth in the 'prone to manipulation' charge. Indeed, the accusation of periodic abuse and misuse of guilt, blame and culpability by church people and theologians is not something that can be easily brushed aside. Nevertheless this quest to rehabilitate sin is paradoxically an extraordinarily positive affirmation of what it means to be human. Despite the keen twentieth-century awareness of the extent to which humankind is conditioned by a myriad of theological, social, cultural and psychological factors, to posit sin is simultaneously to insist on the human capacity to overcome all obstacles. Ironically, the very concept which often stands accused of humiliating human beings has at its core a radical affirmation of each human being's potential to become a free and responsible person and so to discover the grandeur of the human vocation. Such a theological and philosophical vision accepts the human condition as fractured but not destroyed. 'It agrees with Pascal's estimate of humanity as the glory and the scandal of the universe.

It sees all offence as remediable and it locates the remedy in the life, death and resurrection of Christ'.[10]

So sin becomes a reality of the 'heart' of that inner centre of the human person where one chooses freely. Christ did not do away with the law, he protected it by making it more interior by showing the internal sources of evil in the human heart and demanding that these be eradicated (Matthew 5.21–30). The real fault of sin for Jesus is a failure in love of God and of one's neighbour because this kind of love is the fulfilment of the eternal law (Matthew 22.33–40). This means that failure to fulfil the demands of love toward God, others and self is itself a sin. Mere external fulfilment of the law, without love, is hypocrisy (Matthew 25.41–6).

What is important therefore from the point of view of moral good or evil is the free response of the heart, the freely adopted inner attitude that is expressed in one's attitudes. Of course it still remains true that all sin is an 'offence against God', but inner attitude will more often than not be verified in one's action and interaction with fellow human beings with whom God has fully identified by himself taking human form in Jesus Christ. Sin therefore is a failure to share in this loving concern of God for all humankind, which has been shown above all in Christ.

Given then that sin belonged to the interior of the human person, or the 'heart' as the Scriptures metaphorically called it, the question had to be considered as to whether basic options and attitudes were more relevant in determining sinfulness than categorical acts.

Certainly human actions were not understood to be an isolated and disconnected series of good and evil deeds. Instead they were usually expressive of a person's moral character – this basic insight had been accepted since the time of Aristotle. Life was a coherent task, and one moulded one's personality and one's moral character in response to the challenges and important decisions which life held. This forming of character would in turn usually make clear over time the kind of values which the individual had chosen to embrace or indeed to reject as part of his or her 'existential choice'.

The notion of existential choice is largely unproblematic. It is this kind of 'life attitude' that Scripture is referring to when advising that God looks not only at deeds but also at the 'heart' and that he will recreate humankind by giving them a 'new heart' (Proverbs 21.2 and Ezekiel 11.19). This core response or existential blueprint may be somewhat more fluid in youth and adolescence than in the adult years, and there may indeed be some trial and error involved before a core moral personality gradually evolves. This line of reasoning has led some theologians in the latter half of the twentieth century to advance the notion of what is called a 'fundamental option'. They note that each individual's self-commitment transcends individual choices or the sum of them. In the words of Fuchs, 'it underlies them, permeates them and goes beyond them without actually being one of them'. Moral acts are therefore a personal and vital synthesis of the dialectical encounter of those deeper values, which emerge from our very existence and form the backdrop to all moral engagement. This manner of approach, which largely follows the theological anthropology of Karl Rahner and the ethics of Fuchs, Böckle, Demmer and others, attempts to grapple with the exercise of one's core human freedom. It concerns itself, as one author has put it, with the 'background music' to our moral lives and focuses attention on the core stance which underlies all the particular ethical choices we make. In other words, the personal orientation toward good or evil, toward openness or selfishness, toward meaning or nothingness, toward grace or sin and ultimately toward or away from God, is here scrutinized. The moral choices and decisions which one makes are either in harmony or in dissonance with this core stance. It therefore follows that one deepens one's fundamental option when one acts in accord with it and it weakens when our actions are contrary to its thrust.

But how does this concept of sin square with traditional formulations? Moral theology had long made the distinction between grave or mortal sin and light or venial sin. We have noted how this kind of distinction and gradation of sin was already featured in the writings of the Church Fathers. As theological enquiry grew more sophisticated, the subjective condition of the sinner came under ever-greater scrutiny. The question as to whether the sinner has truly been separated from God and definitively lost the divine life of grace by the sinful act or whether it was simply a matter of diminishment of grace or wounding of the relationship with God, became more central. For this reason venial sin came to be seen as a transgression of God's law without 'complete commitment to the evil end' in comparatively unimportant matters or in important matters which were carried out with imperfect knowledge or imperfect consent. Mortal sin, on the other hand, was viewed as 'a decision in radical contradiction to God's will, which always presupposed full knowledge and full consent of the will, and which was usually the case where God's law was transgressed in an important manner'.[11]

Traditional doctrine therefore held that three conditions had to be verified for mortal sin, namely grave matter, full knowledge, and full consent. The shift to a personalist focus led to a re-evaluation of this traditional doctrine. In particular, the emphasis laid on 'the gravity of the matter' was called into question. Was there not a danger that the manualist method had to some extent 'materialized sin', thus glossing over the personal component and the question of basic interior disposition? Besides, was it not really the case that categorical acts are expressive of interior attitudes and it is there that we should first look to determine whether or not sin is present? Catalogues of sin were but 'warnings and indications as to the kinds of behaviour that could lead to the state of mortal, sinfulness, spiritual death'.[12]

Rahner had argued that actions spring from different levels of our being. Not everything we do emerges from or is expressive of our deepest core – the self-disposition of who and what we really are. The human decision-making process for him

> is constructed, as it were, in layers starting at the interior core and becoming more and more external, and because (even free) activations can spring from many different layers . . . it is possible to do one and the same thing and have several, in themselves contradictory, motives and intentions for it.[13]

The difficulty here for Rahner and others was the traditional insistence on identifying mortal sin with one specific act. Was it possible for one specific decision or deed at the outer level to completely alter the interior direction and moral orientation of one's existence?

And so the fundamental option was advanced as giving a more credible anthropological basis to this aspect of the moral life. Mortal and venial sin are held to be expressive of the basic disposition of the sinner. They cannot simply be considered in themselves because choices and deeds evaluated solely by themselves are ambiguous. Mortal sin is therefore any action or series of actions or attitudes that change or is equivalent to changing one's fundamental option toward God. Venial sin, on the other hand, does not concern one's fundamental option at all. It is 'a step not positively directed toward the goal, a step off the main road, but which still leaves a man generally heading toward God'.[14]

We have already seen of course how in Pauline theology sin is never considered an isolated reality in the moral life. Paul speaks of it as the dark force, which resides in the human 'heart' and which is the source of every evil choice and causes human beings to act in a way contrary to that which they know to be right (Romans 7.20–4). Nevertheless, there is a danger that in attempting to correct and compensate for an overly materialist conception of sin, one can unwittingly encourage the opposite fallacy and arrive at an excessively spiritualized notion. Perhaps the temptation of both manualists and casuists to atomize morality by concentrating excessively on the rectitude of individual acts might too easily prompt a tendency to swing to the opposite extreme and minimize the importance of individual choices.

It was fear of this kind of reaction which the 1975 'Document on Sexual Ethics' from the Holy See (*Persona Humana*) sought to highlight when it affirmed:

> In reality it is precisely the fundamental option which in the last resort defines a person's moral disposition. But it can be completely changed by particular acts, especially when, as often happens, these have been prepared for by previous more superficial acts. Whatever the case it is wrong to say that particular acts are not enough to constitute moral sin.[15]

This position has in time been reiterated and explained in greater detail in subsequent documents such as the encyclical *Veritatis Splendor* and the *Catechism of the Catholic Church.*[16] Both documents insist on the importance of evaluating sins according to their gravity and of never losing sight of the sinful character of particular acts, while at the same time allowing that sin runs counter to the 'vital principle' and that there may be a 'proclivity to sin'. Other theological voices, such as those of May and Grisez, have questioned the very usefulness of the fundamental option theory. They argue that it 'needlessly shifts the locus of self-determination from the free choices we make every day . . . to an alleged act of total self-disposition deep within the person that remains pre-reflexive, un-thematic and incapable of being articulately expressed in one's consciousness'.[17] In other words, there is a danger that fundamental option theories will fail to take seriously enough the reality of free choice and the 'self-determining' of the free choices that we make in our daily lives. There is also the problem of opening up an unhelpful and pastorally confusing distinction between mortal sin and grave sin.

Other theologians again, such as Gula, have taken something of a *via media*, or what they refer to as a synthetic view of sin. While acknowledging that there are moments when a concrete action makes the complete reversal of one's fundamental commitment toward the good, this approach also holds that 'actions we judge as sinful must never be taken as abstractions, i.e. as being separated from persons and from an on-going process of inter-action'.[18] In attempting to formulate some kind of synthetic account one might say that mortal sins as individual acts sum up therefore a disintegrating and deteriorating commitment to life and love so as to make real and visible the selfishness that had been slowly festering. In other words, the fundamental option is brought into play through conscious and free decisions. There is, as Grisez has argued, a basic option or commitment for every Christian which consists in living out one's baptismal promises by striving to incarnate the gospel in one's daily life. This is the essential and existential context in which the moral life is lived. Sinful acts are still the expression of a force which is hostile to God and his message. The basic sin therefore continues to be estrangement or alienation from God. But through baptism, Christ's victory over sin is renewed in the 'heart' and with the aid of divine grace one can make a basic decision or fundamental commitment for the moral life in order to mirror the 'image of God' in one's daily existence. This lifelong project must be realized in turn in and through concrete words, deeds and thoughts. Where the notion of a fundamental option is of most value is where it focuses attention on the continuous as well as the immediate dimension of personal moral behaviour. It serves to highlight there the very real struggle within the individual subject between the forces of good and evil. It also recalls the Judaeo–Christian tradition's insistence from the earliest times that sin cannot be understood simply in terms of categorical acts.

In the end the more measured formulations of the fundamental option have sought at once to capture the importance of particular acts and the significance of the larger context within which these individual acts take place. The value of this kind of synthetic view properly understood is that it is a useful corrective to the somewhat atomized foregoing accounts of sin. But it would be counter-productive if this kind of approach were to attempt to separate the fundamental option from concrete kinds of behaviour. This would only contradict the substantial integrity or personal unity of the moral agent in his body and in his soul. In short, those versions of Fundamental Option theory which radically underplay the reality of free choice are to the same extent guilty of underplaying sin itself. They present a picture of the human condition which is ultimately at odds with human self-understanding, as has emerged from both the Judaeo–Christian and Greco–Roman traditions. Mortal and venial sins continue to be meaningful categories and remain essential components of contemporary reflection on sin. They are not in themselves incompatible with the idea of a lifelong path of conversion to God. A renewed theology of sin still requires a system of practical gradation and distinction of sins, but this is now allied to a richer and more profound and personalist anthropology. Sin thus finds its theological place within the context of a personal response to the call of a personal God, and within a community of persons

In summary, we can see that a variety of valuable correctives to the traditional theology of sin have emerged in the latter decades. These have enabled this theology to be more centred on the human person, more genuinely nourished by Scripture and more solidly founded upon a wholesome, integral and truthful anthropology. Nonetheless, the classical insights of Augustine, Aquinas and other great thinkers from the theological tradition on the nature and reality of sin remain valid and indeed essential to any contemporary theological appraisal. These insights are taken more seriously when viewed in the context of the totality of the Christian life-journey. Confined to a narrow literalism, they not only trivialize the question of serious sin but diminish also our understanding of conversion. By appearing to suggest that one might stray in and out of mortal sin on a regular basis, the moral life risks becoming like a kind of board game at which one sharpens one's skills by avoiding sins rather than seeking to deepen one's existential dialogue with Christ.

On the other hand, the passage from mortal sin to real conversion and vice versa involves such a radical re-directing of one's whole life by a fully deliberate choice, that it cannot be an everyday occurrence. It is, in the imagery of St John, the difference between light and darkness. It is a stark choice, an infrequent choice, but nonetheless it remains 'a radical possibility of human nature'.

Notes

1 Gula, R., *To Walk Together Again*, Paulist Press, New York, 95.

2 Haring, B., *Sin in the Secular Age*, St Paul's, Slough, 1974, xii.

3 See Kevin O'Shea's discussion in O'Shea, K., 'The Reality of Sin: A theological and Pastoral Critique', in M. Taylor, *The Mystery of Sin and Forgiveness*, St Paul's, New York, 1971, 95ff.

4 Second Vatican Council, Pastoral Constitution on the Church, *Gaudium et Spes* 13, in Flannery, A., *Vatican II Documents*, Dominican, Dublin, 1981, 903–1000.

5 See Fuchs, J., *Human Values and Christian Morality*, Gill & Macmillan, Dublin, 1970, 82.

6 McCormick, P., *Sin as Addiction*, Paulist Press, New York, 1989, 76.

7 See Xavier Thévenot's engaging discussion of this in Thévenot, X., *Les Péchés: Que peut-on en dire?,* Editions Salvator, Paris, 1992.

8 Williams C., 'Sin and Repentance', in McDonagh, E. (ed.), *Moral Theology Renewed,* Gill and Son, Dublin, 1965.

9 *Gaudium et Spes.*

10 Daly, G., 'Conscience, Guilt and Sin', in Freyne, S., *Ethics and The Christian*, Columba Press, Dublin, 1991, 69.

11 There are scores of definitions to choose from on this topic, these are taken from Peschke, K., *Christian Ethics: Moral Theology in the Light of Vatican II (Vol. 1)*, Goodliffe Neale, Alcester, 1993; Seabury, New York, 1975, 300.

12 Fagan, S., *Has Sin Changed?,* Gill & Macmillan, Dublin, 1978, 71.

13 Rahner, K., 'Some Thoughts on a Good Intention', in *Theological Investigations*, Vol. III, Seabury, New York, 1975, 113.

14 Bockle, F., *Fundamental Moral Theology*, Pueblo, New York, 1980, 96.

15 PH n.10, Congregation for the Doctrine of the Faith Declaration, *Persona Humana* (10), 29 December 1975, Acta Apostolica Sedis (AAS), 68, 1976, 77–96.

16 *Catechism of the Catholic Church*, Veritas, Dublin, 1994

17 See May, W., *An Introduction to Moral Theology,* OSV, Indiana, 1994, 172.

18 Gula, *op. cit.*, 122ff.

5

Of Human Fault, Frailty and Finitude

> Nothing stays for us. This is our natural condition. Yet most contrary to our inclination; we burn with desire to find solid ground and an ultimate sure foundation whereon to build a tower reaching to the Infinite. But our whole groundwork cracks and the earth opens to the abyss. (Blaise Pascal, *Pensées*)

That humankind needs a serious and well-structured system of thought to reflect on human moral frailty and the propensity toward wrongdoing has never been more apparent than in the last half-century or so. Despite some overly optimistic philosophical conjecture that human beings might in some way have moved 'beyond good and evil', the reality was altogether different. The horror of the concentration camps and of the genocide, of ethnic cleansings and worldwide terrorism as well as the ecological rape of global resources have all given ample proof, if such were ever needed, that moral evil is very much a contemporary as well as an historic reality. The philosopher Liebniz superimposed the term 'metaphysical evil' upon the old distinction between moral evil and physical evil. For him, the search for the *raison d'être* of evil must take place within the human creature: 'Because it must be considered that there is an original imperfection in the creature . . . such that it is not capable of knowing all things and that it is prone to error and making mistakes'[1] This of course prompted him to ask a further question as to the existence and intentionality of God: '*Si Deus est, unde malum*?'

Human wisdom had traditionally answered this stark 'Why?' in one of two ways. The stoics (among others), as we have seen, used the 'order' theory. According to this argument evil is in the world in the same way that the part is in the whole. We are a part of a cosmic drama where chaos (evil) is slowly but surely being vanquished by order (good). Evil is therefore not something to be found primordially within humankind, for it precedes the human race. It is not a question therefore of God correcting the evil which man has done, but rather of man gradually effacing the evil which God has allowed to subsist in his creation. Consequently there was no myth of the Fall in the Babylonian or Hellenistic religions and cultural traditions, this kind of explanation was unnecessary because evil was aboriginal. In the *Epic of Gilgamesh* the hero urges his friend Enkidou to join him in combating the evil spirit which guards the Cedar Forest. He tells him 'In the forest the powerful Houmbaba lives; together let us kill him so that we might rid evil from the face of the earth'.[2] The Hellenists likewise, as seen in Hesiod's *Theogony*, held to the theory of 'Double Creation', according to which in the earliest times, chaos – the great abyss, was born alongside the earth which was to be the domain of the 'immortal masters of Olympus'. By contrast, the monotheism of the Hebrews led to a complete change of emphasis. They saw their God as the creator of all things. In this new system creation itself was good, for it proceeded from the divine word and not from some cosmic drama. Evil could no longer be explained with reference to an antecedent chaos – a new myth had to be born. Hence the 'freedom' theory and the Fall. Evil became the overthrowing of divine order not in the cosmic arena but in the human heart. A God who is intelligent and solicitous of human needs had lovingly bestowed order and goodness upon the earth.

On the other hand, it was through the human 'heart' that evil emerged in the world. The old cosmic myths of the Babylonians and the Greeks thus give way to a purely anthropological account. But in giving way they did not totally disappear. Many of the great Christian writers, notably Paul, John and Augustine, took up the notion of the cosmic battle between good and evil, albeit from the standpoint of a creation theology. They used this to great effect in presenting the gospel in a manner which resonated well with the philosophical categories of both the Hellenistic and Roman worlds. But, the framework was metaphysical rather than physical. Man was the author of his own misfortune. The myth of Eden explained how humankind 'willingly corrupted' and 'justly punished' has begotten further pain and further corruption. All human beings bore in some measure the mark and the stain of sin. 'O see in guilt I was born, a sinner was I conceived.'

Hannah Arendt, reflecting on the mental and physic trauma of the survivors of Auschwitz, has spoken of the 'fiction of innocence': 'We who had escaped the hell of camps didn't dare look each other in the eye. Had we the right to be saved? I blush with shame at the idea that I can breathe fresh air while so many of our own died, asphyxiated by gas or burnt alive by the flames'.[3]

To the Jewish and Christian minds freedom implies on the one hand choice and the possibility of doing wrong, and on the other hand guilt – guilt for the wrong which has been done and for the good which has been left undone. Perhaps this is why some of the latter-day psychological explanations of guilt and sin that have limited themselves to the eternal struggle between sexual desire and its repression have proved less than satisfactory. These reduce the moral law ultimately to a series of prohibitions, where in fact it is primarily not so much a prohibition as a command – a command to grow, to develop, to use the gifts of human nature and to choose wisely.

And yet there is a 'fly in the ointment' of human nature that seems to prevent us from fully realizing these possibilities. In some sense, human beings are indeed 'stained' with sin. For Augustine, the situation was relatively clear; every human being born into the world inherits both the *reatus* (the guilt) and the propensity to sin for themselves. He describes this sinful tendency as *concupiscence*. The *reatus* will be removed for those who are baptized but the sinful tendency will always remain. This is what Augustine and subsequent Christian writers understood by the term 'original sin'. The legacy of Adam was therefore guilt and concupiscence. It was not so much that human beings were deprived of free will, for free will remained a quintessential part of the greatness of humankind. But there was a perverse disintegrative and disunifying tendency also which opposed the will of God and right human conduct. Original sin did not come from without: it came from within. Adam chose within his heart to oppose the divine will.

For Augustine, and later for Aquinas, there was what might be called a 'universal voluntariness' about original sin. It was almost as though there were an 'infection' in the human will which brought about estrangement from God and from one's fellow human beings. Generations of thinkers have subsequently wrestled with this idea and its implications for the human condition. Hegel, for instance, seized on the 'alienation' which characterized human beings. Beings who are at once independent, free and autonomous creatures and at the same time subject to internal contradictions and the mutability of the world. Pascal too famously juxtaposed the misery and the grandeur of man. At once capable of soaring to intellectual, aesthetic and spiritual heights, human beings are at the same time liable to the most irrational, selfish and puerile behaviour. Teilhard de Chardin in turn spoke of the disunity or multiplicity, which was at the root of evil. For him the power of Christ was universal, cosmic and reconciling. It was essentially ordered toward drawing all reality into a loving unity. Division, disorganized multiplicity and disunity were symptomatic of evil. 'The multiple produces levels of non-being, pain, and sin, being the traditional dimensions of evil . . . humans embody evil when they strive to stand apart in isolation and refuse selfishly to build up the community of peoples.'[4] In similar vein Tillich spoke of an 'existential estrangement' from the essential realm, and Kant of the human tendency to freely subordinate reason to the emotions. 'Man acts wrongly when he makes love of self the condition for his obedience of the moral law.'[5]

For Paul Ricoeur there is an essential fault in the human person. This fault is expressive of human finitude and is to be distinguished from guilt. Somewhat after the style of Augustine, who had reflected on the restless yearning of the human heart as it awaits its ultimate union with God, Ricoeur points to the human experience of extreme disproportion. For him this is experienced in human action and in the tension between the finitude of character and the infinitude of happiness where character is origin and happiness is infinite end.[6]

The myth of Eden, or, as Ricoeur calls it, the 'adamic' myth, is not only a narrative of origins; it is also, as Vogels has suggested, a Paradise story.[7] It is a world where the creature can dialogue with the creator. Here is not so much an account of something that is past but the story of who we truly are. It is a reflection on our existential situation. Man and woman are engaged with Yahweh, in partnership with Yahweh, in the task of creation. In this analysis, the truth of the Eden myth is not a geographical, historical or literal one: it is existential. The underlying truth that is conveyed in this symbolism is therefore still valid. An invitation is extended to humankind to be in communion with God, with others, and within our very selves so that the world will become a reflection of divine glory. This is a picture of the reconciliation of the yearnings of the human spirit and of the resolution of all tensions between finitude and infinite happiness. God does not create slaves or puppets, he creates instead persons who are called to respond in freedom.

But the Eden myth also demonstrates that it is the human being who in freedom breaks the harmony in refusing partnership with God, and, as the Genesis text emphasizes, all relationships suffer the consequences – relationships with God, with others, with oneself and even with nature (Genesis 3.8–19). God is no longer considered a guardian but a threat. Others are no longer friends but enemies. Even nature has become estranged and is itself, in some respects, hostile now to humanity.

All this is not to say that man is evil; indeed, the constant refrain of the Genesis text is that all of God's creation is good – but there has been a rupture in the dialogue with God. Human beings have gone in search of the infinite, not where it should be sought in the all-good and all-powerful creator, but in the finite capabilities of the creature. This then is the drama which is repeated in the human heart in every instance of sin. The serpent's words suggest a stark choice: 'You will not die . . . But God knows that on the day you eat the fruit your eyes will be opened and you will be like God and have knowledge of good and evil.' The choice is clear; break the relationship of trust with God and open your eyes to a new reality or else remain in your human condition with all its fragility, frailty and ignorance. The temptation is about rejecting faith and trust in favour of knowledge, rejecting belief in favour of sight. In a way it is about substituting the Hellenistic goal (knowledge) for the Hebrew goal (love).

It is no accident that John the Evangelist was to pick up this imagery in the post-resurrection narratives when he recalled Jesus' words to his followers: 'Blessed are those who do not see and yet believe.' Similarly, the disciples racing to the tomb on the first Easter only see . . . emptiness (John 20.8). The sensory powers of the finite creature are of no use before the infinite majesty of God. The appropriate attitude before the Godhead is not one of sight but of belief. As Aquinas was to put it in his immortal hymn: 'Sight is blind before God's glory; faith alone may see his face.' And yet the temptation is great: 'Your eyes will be opened and be like God's.' This is an enticing offer, a one-way ticket out of the prison of the human condition. It is, in effect, the offer of becoming superhuman. To be superhuman though is to be neither human nor divine; it is but a pseudo divinity. Once they have yielded to temptation the eyes of our *proto*-parents are indeed opened – not to an all-encompassing knowledge, but to the pathos of the human condition. They are more shockingly aware than ever before of the gulf that separates humanity from her creator. Xavier Thévenot has drawn a telling comparison between this first 'opening of eyes' in Eden and a New Testament parallel of the disciples on the road to Emmaus. They, too, he reminds us, were entranced by a dream of omnipotence. They had allowed themselves to believe that Jesus, like a magician with a wave of his hand, would resolve all difficulties and do away once and for all with all human limitations. It was of course not so, and Jesus had to help them confront and come to terms afresh with the mysteries of death and failure. In his impromptu commentary on the Law and the prophets he brought them back to a more realistic and authentic understanding of the human story. In a gesture that evoked the invitation of the serpent in Eden he invited them to eat, not with the promise of omniscience this time, but with an assurance of solidarity. There is a new 'opening of eyes' as they were given a glimpse of the risen Lord – but it was a fleeting glimpse. Sight once more had to give way to belief.[8]

The sinful inheritance of Eden, our tradition insists, is not just symbolic in a narrow way: it is also ontological. This is why it is through the new Adam – Christ – that we can reorient our finite lives toward that definitive harmony, that infinite love which only God can give. Ironically, the same principle of solidarity which sees all of the 'children of Adam' share in the transmission of guilt also sees all of the 'body of Christ' share in God's redemptive and merciful grace. The deficiencies in human will are healed and made whole by the *pleroma* of the risen Christ given a desire, on the part of the individual, to respond to this invitation to new life. What is more, the conversion from 'child of Adam' to member of the 'body of Christ' is experienced humanly as a journey – a journey with its successes and failures. That is why Augustine, despite his certainty about the regenerative power of baptism, recognized nevertheless the reality of sinful inclination throughout an entire lifetime. This prompted his distinction between pre-baptismal and post-baptismal concupiscence. Baptism in a sense was a down payment on a new life, which would only be fully experienced in the hereafter.

The reformer Martin Luther was to pick up on this point many centuries later, but, unlike Augustine, he came to identify concupiscence and original sin as one and the same thing. For him, it was no longer simply a question of a sinful disposition but of 'a profound and total upset in the human economy, a physical change in the very substance of the soul whereby . . . man is constituted in a permanent state of sin'.[9]

Although Luther was clear that post-baptismal sin was not imputed, he had a strong sense of the melancholy lot of human beings and a keen awareness of the '*spiritus tristitiae*' that pervades the human heart. He was convinced that human beings couldn't move toward God 'under their own steam'. It was God alone who through Jesus Christ could provide forgiveness and justification. Luther's pessimism about human nature also raised questions about the possibility of achieving moral goodness, about the goodness of God's creation and indeed about the 'freedom theory' *tout court* upon which, in the entire Christian tradition, the very notion of sin and wrongdoing rested. It was these questions which prompted the Council of Trent to refute Luther's ideas in the starkest of terms. Trent defined as anathema the denial of the efficacy of baptism in remitting original sin. For Trent, it was not simply a question of original sin remaining but not being imputed; rather, in baptism the sinner was buried with Christ and so the 'old man' was thrown off and the 'new man' put on. It sought, moreover, to resolve the doubts about the true meaning of original sin by having recourse to the thomistic distinction between 'matter' and 'form': the formal component being the rebellion of the human will against God in the sin of Adam, and the material or matter being the human defects and disorder which subsequently followed.

The merits and demerits of the respective positions of Luther and Trent were to be the subject of much lengthy and detailed historical analysis and need not detain us unduly here. But this episode in the gradually unfolding theology of sin is expressive of a conundrum, which is at the very heart of the human condition. Human beings are at once free and yet somehow a slave to themselves. Convinced of a call to the greatness and to partnership with God, everywhere they are confronted by the signs of their own fragility and finitude. The nature of original sin therefore resonates with the fundamental realization that, as well as individual transgressions and acts of rebelliousness, sins also have a kind of transpersonal and even cosmic dimension. As well as being evidenced in categorical acts, sin at another level also represents the very ground from which these acts spring. Over the years this has been a strong emphasis in the theology of the Reformed tradition, whereas it has been somewhat more understated in Catholic moral theology. Here original sin was more often considered a dogmatic issue and the connection with the moral life was, for the most part, unexplained and undeveloped.

In more recent times there has been a diversity of philosophical and theological reflection on the problem of evil and how humankind experiences it. This is often marked by a tendency to criss-cross the boundaries of philosophy and theology, of the moral and the theologal. Heidegger once memorably drew attention to this confusion of terms in the work of Schelling and to the tendency in European thought more generally to speak of all evil and fault as sin. 'The history of Europe' he observed 'is and remains determined by Christian worldview. Even after the latter is reported to have lost its power; the secularisation of the theological concept of sin and the "christianisation" of the concept of evil and of all related notions seem to go in fact, head in hand.'[10] Perhaps this should not surprise us greatly because the themes we are dealing with here are those which evoke the most profound questions about the meaning of life and the nature of the human condition. These are the perennial human questions, which transcend cultures, creeds and the neat demarcation lines of academic disciplines. Their focus is a thorough reflection on what Kirkegaard has called our chronic 'existential anguish'.

Notwithstanding what has been said earlier about the insufficiency of purely psychological or indeed sociological explications of guilt and fault, one can agree with Kirkegaard that psychology has a role to play in describing and interpreting the attitude of human beings before the mystery of evil, suffering and human limitation. Certainly the psychoanalytic schemas and explanation of original guilt are illuminating in their depiction of sin as an extremely self-centred affair. What is more, the insistence that fear of punishment from an external source cannot form part of a valid conscientious motivation is in broad harmony with, and no doubt has played no small part in, contemporary theology's renewed rejection of legalism. The interdisciplinary work accomplished in recent decades in the fields of ethics and psychology has also contributed substantially to a move toward a more throughgoing and synthetic understanding of the formation of conscience and of its gradual evolution in the individual subject. The behaviourist movement has likewise put Christianity on its guard against ethical behaviour, which owes its origins to conditioning alone.

Both the analytic and behaviourist approaches tend to insist, however, that love of parents and of parental substitutes later in life is a major factor underpinning conscience, guilt feelings, and our acceptance of certain prohibitions.[11] It might be argued that this is a somewhat pessimistic view. The motivation for acting morally is not a positive one such as a commitment to altruism, to generosity or to solidarity with one's fellow human beings; instead it is the essentially negative impetus of retaining affection, goodwill or esteem. Mackey, drawing on the theory of Mowrer among others, concludes that this line of reasoning sees the individual human being as essentially self-centred and self-serving. This is not so much a person-centred as a self-centred morality. This notion of moral action actually approximates more closely indeed to the traditional definition of sin than it does to right moral action. It is clearly at odds with a view which sees love as the defining component, the most basic element in the moral life, where love is understood not primarily in terms of love of the self but as oblative love of the other.

For the Christian view holds that not alone does the agapeic love which we exhibit in our relations with others give expression also in a very real way to our relationship of love with God, but: 'It even contributes to that very freedom which we demand of moral decisions and moral action, by which they are truly moral.'[12] In other words, the moral life is in essence a 'school of love'. Notwithstanding human beings' instinctively selfish motivation toward moral action in the early years, they can and will learn to act lovingly – in the broadest sense of the world – so long as they are open to doing just that. In choosing the loving course they act in a radically free manner, for this is not the kind of action or attitude which can be commanded, demanded or coerced. Of necessity it must be freely given, otherwise it will not be truly love. In short, the truly loving approach is the proof of human freedom and it is only against this backdrop that sin can be properly understood.

All the same, it would be difficult to argue that a personalist other-centred ethical disposition is anything less than strikingly counter-cultural at the beginning of the twenty-first century, at least with regard to the Western world. Much of daily life is lived in a climate of robustly unapologetic consumerism. A popular television commercial currently has well-known personalities from the world of entertainment and sport extolling the merits of a particular cosmetic product. The ad always ends with the remark 'It's brand X and I'm worth it'. Proposing an alternative ethic to the 'I'm worth it' generation will certainly be a tall order. And while one must allow for a necessary and wholesome move away from the excesses of self-effacement and accusations of guilt, which sadly were all-too-frequently features of religious experience for former generations, it would seem that at the dawn of the third millennium there is much evidence of a new narcissism and self-preoccupation abroad.

Certainly the various Christian traditions also have to accept their share of responsibility for a somewhat one-sided emphasis historically on the duties of love toward God and neighbour to the detriment of that wholesome and healthy respect and esteem for self which is implied in Matthew 3.4. (The familiar stereotypes of protestant puritanical humourlessness and of scrupulous, catholic sexual guilt have, no doubt, at least some grain of historical truth.) Modern psychology too has rendered an important service in demonstrating that there is no adequate foundation for entering a mature loving relationship with another, much less with God, until one has arrived at a certain level of self-acceptance and self-respect. In other words, a wholesome love of self is a prerequisite for moral growth.

In speaking of a new narcissism and collective narcissism, however, the focus is not on healthy and necessary self-acceptance but on a marked self-centredness which is prejudicial to, and in certain respects destructive of, interest in others and empathy for them. It implies a preoccupation with self and with self-gratification and admiration. Theissen describes this inordinate self-centredness thus:

> Narcissism is a kind of disunity, for it represents a turning away from others, a turning in upon oneself to the detriment of others. (It) points to a psychological structure that allows for the existence of moral failure and that creates a situation of disunity. The tendency of the human person to withdraw interest in others and to focus it on self is the very core of sin, that is, when the tendency is such that it is freely acknowledged and promoted.[13]

In other words, existential attitudes which were once seen as values such as sharing, generosity, concern for others and altruism lose currency and are viewed as somewhat old-fashioned and, indeed, on occasion, a sign of weakness.

A consumerist social climate will, moreover, augment this tendency because it suggests, sometimes subtly, sometimes crudely, that a person's self-worth will somehow be enhanced or diminished by whether or not they purchase, possess or use a particular product. In short, consumer goods and brands come to be identified with the person and may not be easily substituted. Youngsters growing up today, when asked what they would like for a birthday present, are unlikely to simply ask for jeans, runners and t-shirts *tout court*; they are much more likely to demand Levis, Nikes and Calvin Kleins or whatever the prevailing fashion may be. This in itself of course is unremarkable and not at all indicative of whether a person is generous or selfish, but it is very expressive nonetheless of the kind of commercial climate in which we live today. There was a rather incongruous sight some years ago of a leading fast-food chain opening its first outlet in downtown Moscow amid much fanfare and glittery celebration, while all around people queued for bread and for the daily dietary staples. This was a striking indication of just how far large corporations are prepared to go to achieve global recognition and market dominance. It is hard to imagine that a human being could grow up and live in this kind of competitive commercial climate without being influenced or imbibing at least some of the attendant rhetoric and hype. It would of course be wrong to overstate the materialism of the contemporary world, or indeed to succumb to the same kind of pessimism that we have just criticized in some of the psychoanalytic and behaviourist anthropologies. Human beings are well able to see through the commercial charade of picture-postcard happy families and plastic promises of perfection, but there remains nonetheless a disturbingly self-centred and self-promoting focus at the heart of much modern marketing.

One of the common threads between self-centredness and sinfulness is a mistaken belief in one's self-sufficiency. Theisen calls to mind Niebuhr's observation here that

> The ideal of self-sufficiency, so exalted by our Christian culture, is recognised in Christian thought as one form of the primal sin. For self-love, which is the root of all sin takes two social forms. One of them is the domination of the other life by the self. The second is the sin of isolation.[14]

The problem with the idea of self-sufficiency is that it takes the fundamentally good and noble human desires for self-defence and self-preservation and gives them an inordinate, disproportionate and ultimately false orientation. It is perhaps instructive here to call to mind the two roots for the word 'island' in the latin family of languages. The first, *insula*, has given us the modern term 'insulation' with its emphasis on defence protection and safety. The second term, *isola*, is the root of 'isolation' and connotes loneliness, alienation and estrangement. The old adage that 'no man is an island' may be somewhat hackneyed and clichéd by now; but there is a plain truth here, namely that what insulates also isolates.

All this means of course that discussion of sin is not just a rarefied theological debate for the interested student of history. It has a very real relevance in the contemporary world where it speaks to issues of vital importance such as social alienation and the lack of 'belonging' of *homo urbanus*. There is a delicate balance to be struck in the human heart between the primal instinct for self-preservation and the awareness that to be a human person means *eo ipso* to be at the centre of a complex web of relationships. In more theological terms, what one has to be wary of here is a form of idolatry – an idolatry which puts the self in a position of worship. This is just as surely mistaken as were some of the older spiritualities and more rigorous 'Christian' ideas which put a heavy emphasis on self-abasement rather than self-denial, humiliation rather than humility. Human beings are not gods; they are finite creatures who cannot bear the weight of the infinite. Neither are they mere objects or things, for they are living, rational and moral beings who bear within themselves the image of their divine creator.

Contemporary humankind, at the very moment then in which it experiences the intoxication of progress, also finds itself saddened and disquieted. The real answers to the insatiable yearnings of the human heart have not yet been found and there is instead a new isolation, a sense of being cut off and alone. It is one of the great ironies and indeed tragedies of the modern world that at a time when communications technology is capable of so much interaction, human beings seem to be losing their ability to really communicate. The paradox of the human condition has perhaps never been more apparent then it currently is. On the one hand, we jealously guard our independence, privacy and inner emotions while at the same time knowing that privacy can lead to a lonely isolation which estranges us from our fellow human beings.

This fascination with personal freedom which on the one hand promises liberation and on the other hand only delivers estrangement and alienation is expressive of what the patristic writers called the *incurvatio hominis*. This, as the term suggests, evokes the human being turned in upon himself/herself and away from others. It is what Augustine referred to as the *conversio ad creaturam*. The individualism of Western society certainly allows the individual to become king, independent and sovereign, but it does so at a cost – the cost of being estranged from one's true nature. The freedom which is sought after resembles the water drawn from the well by the Samaritan woman: ultimately it does not satisfy but instead leaves the consumer only craving more. Unable to fully realize one's freedom, Western man is always on the lookout for novel materialist and escapist panaceas to assuage his metaphysical pain. And where for social, economic or any number of other reasons, such materialist panaceas are unavailable, the temptation to seek solace in chemically induced insulation from the world becomes all the greater. It is therefore not all that surprising that youth in the latter years of the twentieth century have been described collectively and, no doubt, somewhat unfairly, as the 'chemical generation'.

The philosophical discipline of ethics and the collective human experience of religion have both lived through image-shattering and iconoclastic moments in recent years. They have emerged weakened and chastened and are now embarked upon the search for a new language with which to engage contemporary quest for meaning. Part of that new language has been the personalist ideal as set forth by Mounier, among others. For them, personalism is not just a new version of individualism as the name might initially suggest. On the contrary, the personalist vision is communitarian by its very nature. 'The person only grows in constantly purifying himself from the individual which is within. One doesn't achieve this by dint of gaining the attention of others but by making oneself available and as transparent as possible to oneself and to others.'[15] For Mounier the primordial experience of the person is the experience of the second person. 'The Thou and the We proceed the I or at least accompany it – one must take this fact, this basic truth as starting point.' Whoever shuts themselves into the 'me' will never find a way out toward discovery of the other and discovery of themselves as persons. Thus whenever communication breaks down or is in some way compromised, one loses one's identity. *Alter devient alienus* – the other becomes a stranger. The individual subject in turn becomes a stranger to himself or herself. This leads personalists to the tentative statement that 'I only exist to the extent that I exist for the other and, in short, to be is to love.'[16] Here, love is understood as *amor amicitiae*, love of the other, love of the ultimate and unique qualities, which make the other human being truly other. This is the other-centred and agapeic love that recognizes the other as person and in some sense loves the other for their own sake. It distinguishes itself from the *amor concupiscentiae* in that it does not have an ulterior motive. On the other hand, when love degenerates from a personalist to an individualist or concupiscent desire it is no longer really love because an ulterior motive has now entered the equation and the other, as Kant would have put it, merely becomes the 'means' of my own satisfaction.

This juxtaposition of the personalist and the individualist views and of the *amor amicitiae* and the *amor concupiscentia* are important in that it emphasizes that sin is not merely a failure in realizing true love. A failure after all could be but a stepping-stone toward a new and stronger relationship. But sin is not only the breakdown of a loving relationship, it also represents in some measure an attempt to construct a substitute universe and to seek after a substitute happiness. Bonhoeffer has observed that whenever human beings reject the goal of personal union with God they tend to place a much higher and unrealistic expectation on the personal relationships that are available to them. The inevitable result is that these too will eventually buckle and perish under the unbearable strain. Schoonenberg goes so far as to suggest that 'a true definition of sin is not verified when we turn away from God, or in the simple *conversio ad creaturam,* the turning toward the creature. It is verified rather in the setting up of idols, that is to say in making creatures attempt to take the place of God'.[17] This of course is the *leitmotif* and the recurrent theme of *the Great Harmartology* of Genesis and Exodus. When human beings forget their 'feet of clay' and seek to put themselves on a par with the almighty their hopes and dreams come tumbling down, just as did the Tower of Babel. Pascal put it altogether more elegantly and simply when he remarked '*Qui veut faire l'ange fait la bête*'.

The Christian vision, and in particular its doctrine of original sin, attempts to shed light on the truth, the sometimes unpalatable truth of who we are. But perhaps it is only in keeping this anthropological verity fixed firmly before us that we have an adequate basis for authentic existence and moral action. It is an approach which is diametrically opposed to the Nietzschean *Zarathustra* who invited his hearers to arise and awaken to the possibilities of the superhuman, to take on the mantle of the master race. Instead, in one respect the starting-point for the Christian is not unlike that of the ancient pagans. It is recalled in the simple legend 'Know thy self' which was once inscribed on the *Delphic* temples. For the Christian, self-knowledge is a bittersweet experience, because it is a reminder of one's finitude and limitation, and yet at the same time it is essential, for this very limitation is the point of encounter and embrace with the Eternal.

Notes

1 Leibniz, *Essays on Theodicy*, Open Court, LaSalle, Illinois, 1985.

2 Azrié, A., *L'epopée de Gilgamesh*, Berg International, Paris, 1979, 53.

3 Arendt, H., 'Letter to the Editor', *Midstream*, Vol. 8 No. 3 (September 1962), 85–7; see also Schneiderman, E. (ed.), *Warsaw Ghetto: A Diary by Mary Berg*, Fischer, New York, 1944.

4 Theissen, J. P., *Community and Disunity: Symbols of Grace and Sin*, St Johns University Press, Collegeville, 1985.

5 Kant, I., *Religion Within the Limits of Reason Alone,* Harper and Row, New York, 1960, 56.

6 Bourgeois, P., *Exstension of Ricoeur's Hermeneutic*, Martinus Nijhoff, 1975, 4; see also Theissen, *op. cit.*, 50.

7 Vogels, W., *Nos Origines: Genèse 1–11*, Montréal, Bellarmin, 2000, 60

8 See Thévenot's excellent commentary on the Genesis accounts in Thévenot, X., *Les Péchés*, Editions Salvator, Paris, 1992, 40–4.

9 Pidanti, A., 'Original Sin', in Pazzolini, P. (ed.), *Sin, its Reality and Nature: A Historical Survey,* Scepter, Dublin, 1964, 147.

10 Heidegger, M., *Schelling* (trans. J-F Courtine), Gallimard, Paris, 1971, 250–1.

11 See Mackey, J. P., 'The Idea of Sin in the Modern World', in O'Callaghan, D., *Sin & Repentence*, Gill, Dublin, 1966, 68ff.

12 *Ibid.*, 69.

13 Theissen, *op. cit.*, 73.

14 See Niebuhr, R., *The Children of Light and the Children of*

Darkness, Scribner & Sons, New York, 1944, 55; quoted in Theissen, *op. cit.*, 85.

15 Mounier, E., *Qu'est-ce que le personnalisme?*, Paris, P.U.F., 1947, 37.

16 *Ibid.*

17 Schoonenberg, P., *Man and Sin*, London, Sheed and Ward, 1965.

6

Solidarity in Sin: The Social Dimension

> When you are harried by day and haunted by night by the fact that you are a Negro, living constantly at tiptoe stance, never quite knowing what to expect next, and are plagued with inner fears and outer resentments: when you are forever fighting a degenerating sense of 'nobodiness' – then you will understand why we find it difficult to wait. (Martin Luther King Jnr., Letter from Birmingham Jail)

We have noted that scriptural accounts of sin have, from the very outset, laid a heavy emphasis on human solidarity and on the communal dimension of sinfulness. Each instance of sin takes its place therefore within the context of human sinfulness. In some sense one can speak of the 'contamination' of evil or the 'pollution' of sin in the world. The prophets too roundly condemned the collective blindness and 'group-egotism' which was prevalent in their society. In the New Testament we see Jesus preaching a message of justice, love, peace and joy to the outcasts, the poor and the sinners, and highlighting some of the hypocrisy and double standards of the religious and social élite of his day. As Segundo puts it, Jesus encountered a world 'turned into a lie, a frozen mental outlook incapable of deeper comprehension'.[1]

In other words, while it is true that there is a very

pronounced development of the sense of personal culpability and responsibility throughout the Judaeo–Christian Scriptures, it is equally true that the sense of sin as a social reality never diminishes. The biblical vision is an integral one, giving a multidimensional picture of humankind. To be sure, the *dramatis personae*, the original sinners of the Eden myth, are an individual man and an individual woman; but as the solution story unfolds we find a couple, a family, a dynasty, a city, an entire nation, indeed all of humanity, described, in some sense, as sinful. Some of the great kerygmatic and prophetic texts such as Isaiah 1–5, Deuteronomy 4–7 and Matthew 23–7 are clearly addressed to and descriptive of the totality of humanity in both its personal and social dimensions. Careful emphasis is laid on the responsibilities, for instance, held by people in different roles and functions, heads of families, civic leaders, parents and religious leaders. Similarly, the divine word denounces the misdeeds and uncharitable dispositions of all manner of groups and assemblies. Indeed, the evolving 'education of conscience' which can be traced across the historical unfolding of the Scriptures represents a pedagogical advance which never sacrifices the sin's social dimension to the personal or *vice versa*. Gently the people of God are led to assume, distinguish and articulate the responsibilities that belong on the one hand to individuals and on the other to groups and indeed to the multiple collective expressions of humankind: families, clans, tribes, tongues, peoples and nations. Amid all this great diversity of historical and social forms, the preaching of the law of the Covenant is designed to engender at once individual responsibility and community solidarity.

The Gospels, which in turn present the 'fulfilment of the Law and the prophets', make abundantly clear the close parallel between, on the one hand, 'hardness of heart' and, on the other, the 'perversity of the world'. This double symbolism lies at the heart of the concept of sin in the Bible. Before the resplendent revelation of God in and through his son Jesus Christ, the very kernel of sin as a *violence fratricide et déicide* is laid bare.[2]

The animated debates on the Sabbath, the pure and the impure, the precepts of the law, table fellowship with sinners, all expose a collective hardness of heart among the scribes, Pharisees and lawyers, and reveal what comes to be called 'the sin of the world'. It is sin born in the human heart, born in the hearts of the learned, those who 'know' much but 'understand' little. This is understood to take expression in the very life of the group. That is why Jesus is able to warn his followers to be on their guard against the 'yeast of the Pharisees'. Even though the refusal to open one's eyes and one's heart to his saving message is individual, the structures, the social ties and pressures are such that the Pharisees appear to embody a particular, single attitude.

In the fifth chapter of John's Gospel Jesus, reacting to criticism by the Jewish leaders of his cures at the Sheep Gate Pool on the Sabbath, rounds on the Pharisees collectively, telling them that they do not have God's word abiding in them. On another occasion he warns how hard it is for Pharisees to convert to the good news and how difficult it is for the rich man to enter the kingdom of heaven. Later still he reminds both the scribes and Pharisees that they have taken the Law of Moses – the noble heritage of the people of Israel – and made of it a tissue of merely human customs, practices and institutions.

That said, Jesus is clearly not clumsily 'tarring all with one brush' here. He is highlighting instead the sinful mentality, which can and does take hold within the dynamics of a group where no one has the courage to speak up. Sin, as Schoonenberg and others have observed, is more than the accumulation of individual acts of sinfulness; it is, as St Paul writes, a power which fights for dominion over our lives. 'Sin abounded . . . sin hath reigned' (Romans 5.20–1).

The inward disruption of the sinner is mirrored in the dismemberment of society. For Paul, sin has a very real corporate dimension. In virtue of baptism the individual is admitted to the community, the *Koinonia* of the body of Christ: thenceforward he or she cannot merely be considered an individual, nor can their acts, attitudes and dispositions be a solely private concern. 'None of us lives to himself and none of us dies to himself' (Romans 24.7). All are members of the body of Christ. Just as it is in and through the people of God that the individual is sanctified, so too the solidarity of the people of God is injured by 'individual' sin.

Perhaps because of the rampant individualism and fragmentation of modern life in the Western world, this biblical conviction of the corporate aspect of sin has been taken up anew in recent decades. Theologians have scrutinized at length the 'privatization of sin' or the 'privatizing morality' which laid inordinate emphasis on the need to 'save one's soul' to the detriment of opening one's eyes to the social embodiment of sin.[3] The basic anthropological question as to whether the human being is to be considered merely an individual unit according to sociological and political and economic conventions is the focus of their interest here. Is he or she a single entity or is this in fact a person who only achieves his or her fullness in communion and relationship with the other?

To the Christian worldview this question is all-important because personal distinctiveness forms the very image of God in humanity. It is the mode of existence shared by God and man. As a contemporary orthodox theologian has put it, it is 'the ethos of Trinitarian life imprinted upon the human being'.[4] If this is so then the relational dimension, the existential call to realize oneself, is a relationship of love and communion with the other: it is not some form of appendage, it is integral to the human situation. Similarly the social dimension of sin can never be construed as some kind of afterthought, for it is an essential component of the '*mysterium iniquitatis*'. To be a relational being means that the human person cannot achieve his or her true realization except in communion with the other. Sin is an egocentric act or attitude, therefore, because it is a refusal to open the 'heart', to reach out and to love.

For the very same reason, however, sin radically contradicts respect for the other, for the ideals of justice and for the common good which are the very hallmarks of communion and community. All sin therefore, whether committed in secret or in the open, has a collective dimension. Levinas tellingly observes:

> From the moment the other looks at me, I am responsible for them. Without yet having taken responsibility, their responsibility is laid upon me . . . before the other the I becomes infinitely responsible . . . in the phrase of Dostoevsky, 'We are all guilty of everything before everyone and I more so than others.'[5]

Sin therefore is in some sense an existential failure, a failure with regard to existence and life and the demands of growth, development, interaction and responsibility, which are ours in virtue of being human persons. Viewed in this way, sin is the seed of division and fragmentation which runs counter to the growth of the communion and the building up of the body of Christ. The ecclesial community has, after all, a mission to be the efficacious sign of the love of God at large and at work in our world. Everything which is contrary to that love therefore, and which bears the marks of selfishness, envy, pride and everything which is turned in upon itself, even that which is done in secret, is a betrayal of that ecclesial calling to make manifest the image of the one and triune God.

For the same reason one might argue that the divisions between Christians is rightly called a scandal. If the Church sees herself as a 'kind of sacrament or sign of intimate union with God and of the unity of all mankind . . . and . . . an instrument for the achievement of such union and unity'.[6] then there is something seriously amiss in the divisions within the Christian family. And so to the extent then that Christians have been unable to realize the true unity which Christ prayed for at the hour of his passion 'that they may all be one' (John 17.21), they bear witness in effect to the dismemberment of the body of Christ. One might say too that in bearing witness they also bear a certain collective responsibility. The people of Israel had a very profound sense of their common responsibility because of the collective character of the pact, the covenant, which bound them to Yahweh. In a similar way the people of the New Alliance are to be acutely conscious of their intimate and collective union with the risen and glorified Lord in the body of Christ and of their call to make this union apparent in the here and now. The New Testament clearly affirms the universality of sin and the universal responsibility of all for it, as well as the universality of the call to salvation. In John's Gospel particularly, Jesus challenges the prevailing view that sin is specific to a particular family, or blood line, or concrete event; and so, when asked, 'Rabbi, who sinned, this man or his parents, that he was born blind?' Jesus replies, 'It was not that this man sinned, or his parents, but that the works of God might be made manifest in him' (John 9.2—3). He thus repudiates a narrow, restrictive understanding of solidarity in sin which sees it in some sense as restricted to the confines of the clan or tribe and instead challenges his listeners to open their eyes to the signs of sin all around. Again and again he overturns and upsets the conventional notions of sinfulness which had conveniently confined sin to particular segments of society – the Gentiles, the lepers, the publicans, the women who strayed beyond the strict societal role allotted to them. He proposes instead a much wider understanding of the sin which is in every human heart and which does not respect the boundaries of caste or creed, age or status, role or religion.

Yet all this is done in tandem with and in the context of the portrayal of God as gracious and compassionate. Fuellenbach describes Jesus' table-fellowship with outcasts and 'sinners' as the 'action parable revealing the compassionate God, who desires to embrace all human beings in one great community of brothers and sisters.'[7] As the fourteenth-century English mystic Julian of Norwich put it, 'We have been loved . . . from before the beginning.' So the love which Jesus shares with his table fellows is in fact the same love which carries and sustains the life of the world from one moment to the next. In him we are given a clear image of God's love which reaches out toward all creation. The Wisdom of Sirach puts it somewhat more succinctly and simply: 'the compassion of the Lord is for every living thing' (Sirach 18.13). In other words, God's love embraces the entire cosmos.

Conversely, whenever human beings turns their gaze inward, whenever they yield to the temptation of self-advancement at the expense of others, whenever they strain or sever the ties that bind them to their fellow human beings, the image of God's love is in the same measure obstructed and obscured. If this is so then the Good News is nothing less than a call to solidarity. Communities are brought into being by the participation of individual men and women, responding to the divine impulse towards social relationships – essentially the impulse to love and to be loved – which was implanted by the God who created them. It is a distortion of human nature, then, to suppose that individuals can exist independently of society as if it had no demand upon them. Solidarity is a theologal value – and indeed a moral imperative – precisely because it is reflective of a God who is in solidarity with his people. Our experience of this God pushes us, in turn, toward an awareness of our obligation to be in solidarity with our fellow human beings.

From this perspective, the story of salvation is the progressive revelation of a God who enters into the world of men and women so that they too can enter into the world of their fellow men and women. Solidarity therefore expresses itself as a practical expression of the communion which is between God and humanity and which is made possible through the death and resurrection of Christ. The mystery of the Church is a participation in the Trinitarian life of God. Divine reality is therefore the basis for communion in the Church and for solidarity in the world. Solidarity, in other words, is the recognition of the communion of the single human family into which all are born. This indeed is the freshness and the force of the biblical message. The good Samaritan, someone who does not belong to the right group, the true religion, or the proper country exhibits the solidarity that Jesus proposes as a model to be followed. It is the attitude of someone who has crossed over demarcation and boundary lines. This solidarity is not abstract, theoretical or ideological. It is universal. It entails an opening of oneself to the other person and to their needs and allowing one's heart to be touched to the point of doing whatever is necessary to come to their aid. Solidarity cannot therefore be just a sentiment, it has to be an engagement of the person, a praxis, which is stripped of all self-seeking and governed by the seeking out of what is necessary for the other.

> Solidarity is not a feeling of vague compassion or shallow distress at the misfortunes of so many people both near and far. On the contrary, it is a firm and persevering determination to commit oneself to the common good; that is to say to the good of all and of each individual because we are all really responsible for all.[8]

But the parable of the good Samaritan demonstrates that in addition to the possibility for positive and creative solidarity as exhibited by the central figure, there also exists the possibility of a negative and destructive solidarity as borne out in the conduct of the priest and the Levite. They have become so concerned with the possible ritual impurity of the 'corpse' before them that they pass by, blind to their neighbour in need, oblivious of the life which is still within him. The little episode on the road to Jericho neatly encapsulates and depicts the collective sinful mentality. The priest and Levite have become so entrenched, so blinkered by their circumscribed world of closed options, set judgements and guaranteed conclusions that they are literally blind to the other and to his need. True solidarity, on the other hand, has to emerge out of an honest attempt to mirror the love of God for us in our lives and out of a vision of the transcendence and unity of all things in Christ.

The point here of course is that solidarity in love and solidarity in sinfulness are just two sides of the same coin. All are called to the fullness of existence, which is the life of the Trinity, a life of personal coherence and communion in love. But there is everywhere evidence of disunity, spiritual division and fragmentation. Maximus the Confessor once dramatically described it thus:

> Sin smashed nature into a thousand pieces, although God made it and wished it to be one, so that mankind instead of being a harmonic whole, is become a multitude of warring individuals who often rend each other like wild beasts.'[9]

A social dimension of sin is therefore beyond doubt since it is but the expression of the moral failure of human beings to fully realize those relationships which ultimately gives them life and love. One can therefore easily understand the notion of collective egotism and readily chart the social consequences of sin.

Theologians today increasingly point to another expression of sin in the form of 'sinful structures'. The suggestion is that somehow sin can become institutionalized in the structures, laws and customs of society. In theological terms, 'structural sin' refers here to the social objectification of sin. It describes the embodiment of sin in structures, which in turn produce further disvalues in the form of intolerance, inequality and all manner of injustice. This kind of language affords us a theological perspective that broadens our vision beyond consideration of moral fault and failure within interpersonal relationships toward a discernment of the effects of sin within the very fabric of society. It also urges an evaluation of sin and attentiveness beyond what Ricoeur calls *relations courts* or immediate relationships. It encourages an examination of those societal instruments and organisms which nurture, maintain and multiply injustice.

The continuing development of social ethics generally, and of Catholic social teaching particularly, has led to a renewed focus on key political and socio-economic relationships and structures. Up until the Second Vatican Council there was no reference to the term 'social sin' in magisterial documents. Indeed the Council itself refrained from using the term. The constitutional document however did get to the nub of the matter when it observed:

> To be sure, the disturbances which so frequently occur in the social order result in part from the natural tensions of economic, political and social forms. But at a deeper level they flow from man's pride and selfishness, which contaminate even the social sphere. When the structure of affairs is flawed by the consequences of sin, man, already born with a bent toward evil, finds these

> new inducements to sin, which cannot be overcome without strenuous efforts and the assistance of grace.[10]

As church bodies and non-governmental organizations became increasingly involved in the integral development of under-developed regions and nations, so too fresh attention was given to the obstacles, infrastructural barriers and institutionalized blockages which impeded their progress toward this goal. CELAM, the Latin American grouping of Catholic Bishops' Conferences, was very much to the fore in this kind of analysis. At their gathering in Medellín, Columbia in 1968, they committed themselves to tackling unjust structures and institutionalized violence.

> In many instances Latin America finds itself faced with a situation of injustice that can be called institutionalised violence when, because of a structural deficiency of industry and agriculture, of national and international economy of cultural and political life. Whole towns lack necessities and live in such dependence as hinders all initiative and responsibility as well as every possibility for cultural promotion and participation in social and political life.[11]

The bishops were acknowledging here in a detailed way the view that sin and its effects become embodied in structures, social relationships and even in collective attitudes, political systems and philosophical worldviews. The repeated use of the term 'structural' in the final document is quite striking, as is the fact that unjust conditions are sometimes described as 'situations of sin'.

All the same, these reflections are by no means a rejection of traditional theological reflections on sin. The bishops are careful to note the personal origins of sin and the central thrust of the Christian message as a call to conversion. For them, such a conversion must also be translated into profound changes in social structures. A decade later, Pope John Paul II, on his visit to Mexico, reminded his listeners at the shrine of Nuestra Señora de Zapopan that Mary would help them overcome the multiple 'structures of sin' in which their daily, personal, family and social life was immersed.[12] The observation opened the way for the final *Puebla* document to develop the theme at some length. In so doing it made repeated reference to the 'situation of sin' which in one way or another touches the lives and daily activity of all people.

Two years later the 1971 Synod of Bishops, which had as its theme 'Justice in the World', spelt out the relationship between personal sin and social structures. The synodal statement expressed concern for 'those who suffer violence and are oppressed by unjust systems and structures' (n. 5) and noted that 'education demands a renewal of heart, a renewal based on the recognition of sin in its individual and social manifestations' (n. 51). Subsequently, the 1984 *Apostolic Exhortation on Reconciliation and Penance* dedicated an entire chapter to 'personal sin and social sin'. The document emphasizes that 'sin in the proper sense is always a personal act' (n. 16) and that social sin is a valid way of looking at the 'accumulation and concentration of many personal sins'.

Social sin therefore has an analogical meaning because it allows us to examine the sinful situation in its 'structural and institutional aspects', while at the same time bearing in mind that 'at the heart of every situation of sin are always to be found sinful people'. Clearly the document was concerned that the notion of social sin should not be contrasted with personal sin but seen rather as a necessary and logical extension of it. It foresaw a danger that in ascribing some form of stand-alone status to the concept of social sin, one might actually diminish the notion of personal sin and with it the idea of personal guilt and personal responsibility. If the link to personal guilt was severed then the whole question of human freedom and responsibility was also severely compromised and relativized. There would emerge then a rather bleak and pessimistic view of the world in which humanity was more or less, to use the phrase of Augustine, a '*massa damnata*'. Where individual people or indeed groups of people did not accept responsibility for sinful situations, then no real conversion was possible and the situation would quite literally be hopeless.

So even though the Christian insistence on the human capacity for sin and responsibility for sin has sometimes been derided and scorned as portraying an altogether too pessimistic view of human nature, the converse is in fact the case. The insistence on the human capacity for sin is therefore just another way of making a positive statement on human liberty. Human beings are not mere puppets who succumb to all kinds of psychological, cultural and societal pressures. To be sure, all these can and do influence our activity and attitudes, but in the vast majority of cases they do not completely erase personal responsibility. To deny personal responsibility would be 'to deny the person's dignity and freedom which are manifested – even though in a negative and disastrous way – in this responsibility for sin committed'.[13] Besides, there is always the danger 'of shifting the cause of evil ever more to external, social conditions and to forget about the evil in man's own heart'.[14] The papal *Exhortation On Reconciliation and Penance* was at pains therefore to recognize in 'the clearest and most unequivocal way' the 'disastrous conditions' and 'intolerable situations' brought about by sinful social situations. It acknowledged the traditions, institutions and societal mechanisms and mentalities which have been contaminated by sin, but at the same time cautioned against attributing all guilt and blame to impersonal structures. Social institutions and mechanisms are man-made, so the reform and recreation of social institutions must go hand in hand with true *metanoia* and conversion of the human heart.

The 'signs of sin' which, despite depending ultimately on human responsibility, are manifest in mechanisms that are 'relatively independent of human will', are discussed again in the 1986 instruction *On Christian Freedom and Liberation* from the Congregation for the Doctrine of the Faith. The language here represents a subtle but significant shift in emphasis and prepares the way for a more detailed analysis in the aforementioned *Sollicitudo Rei Socialis.*[15] That document sought to confront the question of 'sinful structures' in a particular way. It was the first time that the universal magisterium used this concept directly[16] and the development was significant because, although expressions such as 'social sin' and 'unjust structures' had already found their way into the social teaching, the phrase 'structures of sin' had not previously gained official recognition. The term was understood to indicate 'the existence of structures, which are historical "objectifications" of sin's social dimension, almost like "places" where it is present and effective'.[17] Among the reasons listed by the document for such structures being described as sinful were opposition to the will of God, to the common good, and to the recognition of the other as neighbour. At the same time there was careful emphasis that sinful structures are 'always linked to the concrete acts of individuals who introduce these structures, consolidate them and make them difficult to remove.'[18]

For many contemporary theologians the reality of sinful structures is not only demonstrable in its dehumanizing expressions in terms of social injustice and social inequality; it is also observed in various prevailing mentalities or 'fundamental temptations' which conspire to maintain the sinful scenario and thus to impede the building of a better society.[19] Among these is an 'attitude of resignation' which either underplays the very reality of the evil which is present or else declares it to be absolutely impossible to overcome. The long-term effect of this kind of stance is a selective vision, which is in fact blind to the inequity and institutionalized evil that are ever present. Of course tacit complicity and the desire to avoid one's share of responsibility also reinforce this. There is always the temptation to hide behind the defence that the 'system is always right' and to simultaneously demonize some groups and individuals.

A second mistaken mentality is that of 'taking refuge in the private'. This is the not altogether uncommon tendency across the various Christian traditions of drawing sharp demarcation and indeed exclusion lines between the social sphere and the sphere of faith and morals. The 'privatizing moral stance' has been a well-documented and critiqued phenomenon over the years. This kind of stance affords the individual the possibility of a certain ethical ambiguity – not to say double-think – in for instance defending human rights on the one hand while ring-fencing all other aspects of faith and morality as private property.

A third and final sinful mentality is what one might call the temptation to 'take refuge in strategic measures'. This is a kind of *via media,* which acknowledges the need to make certain strategic remedial intentions without calling into question the entire social edifice. Here a certain recognition of injustice and imbalance is forthcoming, as well as an admission that 'something must be done' but such remedial measures will always be carried out within the logic and ethos of the existing system, thereby reinforcing that very system and the underlying idolatry. This idolatry, according to the social encyclical, is not only witnessed in the attitudes of individuals; it is also the frequent stance of 'nations and blocs.'[20]

Real transformation of structures of sin requires a much more profound approach, which in the Judaeo–Christian tradition has always been referred to as conversion. Conversion here is not about switching religious affiliation but about turning the heart back toward God alone. If conversion is not to fall foul though of this same privatizing tendency it must be understood not only as an interior reality but also as an external and relational enterprise. True conversion is at once interior and exterior. It is not just 'substantially' an interior reality which somehow also expresses itself in external relationships. In theological terms conversion belongs to a person's relationship with Christ. In conversion one expresses one's moral personality in the concrete and positive exercise of human freedom. In a sense the entire life of discipleship – the entire *Sequela Christi* – can be seen as a continuous conversion. Looked at in this way conversion is essentially about the construction of the kingdom of God.

Or again, if justice is about right relations, then conversion, which is about the realization, the incarnation of this kingdom value, implies the healing and restoration of all relationships. Structures of sin must therefore become structures of grace, of salvation of justice and ultimately of agapeic love. This can only be brought about through the new awareness of human interdependence and a 'firm and persevering determination to commit oneself to the common good'. Such an awareness and commitment are, according to the aforementioned social encyclical, expressive of that fraternal and social virtue which we call solidarity. This kind of solidarity in turn bespeaks a determination to go beyond cosmetic change, to reject maudlin *via media* mentalities and commit oneself to the core kingdom values of justice, peace and the integrity of all creation. To say that justice and freedom must come first is not necessarily to opt for violent opposition to present oppression with its inherent violence. It may be to refuse to opt for a cheap reconciliation that permits the destruction and oppression to continue.[21] In other words, it is the task of Christianity, and more particularly of ethics and of prophecy, to render the invisible sin visible. But such a task is always easier said than done. Each of us has what Schoonenberg described as a 'situated freedom'. It is only by a slow and gradual process therefore that one gains the wisdom, insight and strength to transcend, critique, and, if necessary, reject the prevailing values of one's own culture.

It is one of the tasks of theologians and believers more generally to illustrate the complexity of the symbiotic relationship, and interdependency, between the person and society and the necessity of developing an integral language and praxis for combating sin in all its expressions. In so doing one must be careful not to imply determinisms that would eliminate personal moral agency. This caveat has been a constant feature of social teaching and has most recently found expression again in the *Catechism of the Catholic Church.*[22] Commenting for instance on the reflections of Pope John Paul II in this area one analyst has noted

> In his own encyclicals and apostolic exhortations, as well as in the CDF documents he invokes, there is strong and justified suspicions of terms such as 'systemic evil', 'structural sin', 'social guilt' and so forth. Such expressions, which are found chiefly in the language of the ideological left, obscure the 'person-sized' scale of moral warfare. They also provide, as the Pope says, 'specious reasons' by which individual people excuse themselves from moral responsibility for the wrongs of the world.[23]

A useful corrective to this tendency may be found perhaps in the Johannine notion of the 'world' as a meditation on the interplay between the two experiences of sin, namely the 'reign of sin' on the one hand and the 'sinful act' on the other. Although the world owes its origin and being to the divine word, nevertheless it has been judged for 'the world lies in the power of the Evil One' (1 John 5, 19). The stance of human beings before the world is therefore one of choice. John's notion of the 'world' and what it 'has to offer' gives us then a basis for reflection on the dynamic of sin which every human being experiences. There is no doubt that more scholarship and analysis is needed of the symbiotic relationship between personal sin and the structural embodiments of that sin in society. It is a task not only for ethicists and theologians but also for those with expertise in the human and social sciences. The question of 'social sin' undoubtedly remains one of the theological issues, which would most gain from thorough-going and far-reaching interdisciplinary research.

In the meantime the Church must give renewed emphasis to the distorting effects of sin within the human community: in particular, those distortions to the relation of mutuality and equality which give rise to domination and subordination and thereby obscure the imprint of the divine creator on human existence have to be brought to light. There is also a need to collectively work toward a truly transformative and liberating solidarity, an attitude that sees doing justice as constitutive of Christian faith. 'Because God has identified himself with all persons through the covenant, especially with the "least brethren" and because every person is a true image of God, response to God in faith and response to neighbour in love and solidarity are inseparable.'[24]

Human sinfulness and finitude will always make the historical realization of justice, and by extension the removal of structures of sin, only imperfect and at best partial. This is reflective however of the eschatological nature of Christian faith. By definition, the work of justice solidarity, and individual and collective conversion, is a task for life. There is always more to be done in bringing about the transformation of society from the old 'order of sin' into the new 'order of grace' just as, in Pauline terms, there will always be more to do in 'putting on the new man' and 'taking off the old'. The alternative to this kind of vision of social praxis and solidarity is an inherently selfish and pessimistic view, which refuses to accept that the reality of sin in the world, both individual and social can be modified, and indeed overcome, through the grace of Christ. To wish to safeguard, protect and maintain social reality and existence as it is means to endorse, however unwittingly, a social situation that is glaringly sinful. It is, more often than not, to acquiesce unconsciously in sin.[25]

Evangelization, which is the proclamation of the Father's love and discipleship, the incarnation of the Son's good news, takes place in the *communio* of solidarity where fraternal love finds expression in the sustenance of the Holy Spirit. This deep reciprocal relationship between evangelization, discipleship and solidarity occurs first and foremost at a practical level in the real lives and hearts of Christian people. This is where true conversion is effected. It consists not only in identifying one's complicity in social sin and confessing that complicity but also in turning toward, and committing oneself to, the values of justice and peace and the integrity of God's creation. But this is never something done in isolation: it is always done as a human person at the centre of a network of relationships. In and through the dialectical interaction of the individual and the collective, the value-laden, affect-laden structure, which we call society, is gradually constructed. The individual does not necessarily have any real consciousness of having taken part in the construction process, and yet this 'massively intractable objectivity' is in fact put together by people and has its roots in the behaviour and habits, traditions and prevailing ideas of human beings.[26]

Conversion of the heart then means that Christians are to be socially engaged. They make use of the very same dialectic and dynamism which can be a vehicle for the logic of sin, and seek to make of it instead a vehicle for the logic of grace. Consequently, conversion is really about a complete overhaul, a turning over or transformation. It is the task of disciples of Christ to work to help make this transformation real. Concretely this is done by strategies which encourage turning away from selfishness and self-centredness, and toward other-centredness.

Paul once memorably summarized the task thus: 'Let each of you look not to your own interests, but to the interests of others. Let the same mind be in you that was in Christ Jesus, who . . . emptied himself . . . and became obedient to the point of death – even death on a cross' (Philippians 2.4–8). More than ever, Christians need to realize that conversion should be expressive of solidarity, and that social institutions and structures are not just extrinsic or marginal factors but that they enter determinatively into the composition of one's moral ideas and the concrete reality of one's moral life. Only in this way will sinful social structures ultimately be transformed and healed.

But this need not be seen as some form of utopian vision. Events of recent years such as the collapse of the totalitarian systems of government in Eastern Europe, the unravelling of apartheid and the significant, albeit painstakingly slow, successes of peace processes in Northern Ireland and South Africa are real signs of hope. They bear eloquent testimony to the fact that people do transform and transcend divisive societal structures, which once seemed set in stone. Born out of genuine and integral conversion, the stance of solidarity is the antidote to the social embodiment of evil. It is the moral virtue and social attitude which best corresponds to the reality of human interdependence at a local and global level while bearing witness to the fact that liberating salvation comes from God and is effected ultimately by God alone. Solidarity might be summarized as 'the sentiment which for two thousand years has lived in the soul of the Church' inspiring humankind toward 'creating the social conditions, capable of offering to everyone possible a life worthy of man and of a Christian'.[27]

A final thought on the social embodiment of sin is prompted by Ricoeur's observation that when we attempt to deal with the facts of sin we discover a kind of coded language which speaks only indirectly through metaphor, symbol and imagery. The social expression of sin is frequently referred to in the vocabulary of contamination and despoilment. There may well be a possibility here of developing afresh a metaphor which we have described in its original biblical context as being pre-moral and which had in that context too narrow an identification with sexual impurity. We have already seen how the Jewish mind had a strong sense of the things which rendered a person unclean. The language of stain in a more contemporary setting does have the potential to shed light on the allure of sin, which makes it a powerful and deadly social contaminant. The laws of Leviticus regarded moral evil as a defilement of the person, which could be achieved through simple, even casual, contact. Likewise two of the protagonists in the parable of the good Samaritan used this as an excuse for not responding to human need. Looked at in another way, the very same metaphor of stain is but an echo of Paul's observation 'that all have sinned and fallen short of the glory of God'. It is symbolic in some way of our 'solidarity' in sin.

There is here a common starting point, an acknowledgement that none of us can close our eyes to the social expressions of sin, that being embroiled in a relational world we have all internalized attitudes which sully ourselves, others and our relationship with God. To be human is to be embroiled in the consequences of sin 'before one has the means to object'.[28]

Notes

1 Segundo, J. L., *Evolution and Guilt*, Orbis, New York, 1974, 55.
2 See Pinto de Oliveira, C. J., 'Péché Collectif', *Lumiére et Vie*, December 1987, 55ff., to whom I am indebted for this scriptural analysis.
3 See, for instance, Moses, A. and Leers, B., *Moral Theology: Dead Ends and Ways Forward,* Burns & Oates, Kent, 1990, 24–5.

4 Yannaras, C., *The Freedom of Morality,* St Vladimir's Press, New York, 1996, 23.
5 Levinas, E., *Ethique et Infini* (ed. Fayard), Paris, 1982, 104–5 and *passim.*
6 LG 1, Second Vatican Council, Dogmatic Constitution on the Church, *Lumen Gentium*, in Flannery, A., *Vatican II Documents*, Dominican, Dublin, 1981, 350–440.
7 Fuellenbach, J., *The Kingdom of God: The Message of Jesus Today,* Orbis, New York, 1995, 177.
8 SRS 38, John Paul II Encyclical Letter *Sollicitudo Rei Socialis* (30 December 1987) (SRS), 38.
9 *Quaestiones ad Talassium.* 2 P.G. 90, 272, in AAS 80 (1988), 513–86.
10 *Gaudium et Spes* 25; see also O'Keefe, M., *What Are They Saying About Social Sin*?, Pacifist, New York, 14ff., where there is a useful summary of developments in this area
11 The Conference of Bishops of Latin America, *La Iglesia en la Actual Transformación de America Latina,* Imprenta Mexicana, Mexico, 1970, 16.
12 See Javier Galdona's excellent summary of recent magisterial developments in Fuček, I., *Il Peccato Oggi,* PUG Rome, 1991, 219–37.
13 Apostolic Exhortation *Reconciliato et Poenitentia* (16), 2 December 1984, in AAS 77 (1985), 213–17.
14 Peschke, K., *Christian Ethics: Moral Theology in the Light of Vatican II*, Goodliffe Neale, Alcester, 1993; Seabury, New York, 1975, 307–10.
15 *Sollicitudo Rei Socialis* 36ff.
16 *Ibid.*
17 Bastianel, S. *et al.*, *Strutture di Peccato*, Piemme, Milano, 1989, 15ff. (my own translation).
18 *Sollicitudo Rei Socialis* 36 and *Reconciliato et Poenitentia* 16.
19 The list of sinful mentalities, which I have presented here, is taken from Bastianel (*op. cit.*).
20 *Sollicitudo Rei Socialis* 37.
21 McDonagh, E, *The Gracing of Society*, Gill & Macmillan, Dublin, 1989, 91.
22 *Catechism of the Catholic Church*, c. 1869.
23 Neuhaus, R. J., '*Solicitudo* Behind the Headlines', in Myers, K. A. (ed.), *Aspiring to Freedom,* Eerdmans, Michigan, 1988, 153.
24 Hollenbach, D., *The Faith that Does Justice*, Paulist, New York, 1977, 225.
25 Lane, D., *Foundations for a Social Theology*, Paulist, New York, 1984, 78ff.
26 Kierans, P., *Sinful Social Structures*, Paulist, New York, 1974, 74ff.
27 *Catechism of the Catholic Church*, c. 1942.
28 See Suchocki, M. H., *The Fall to Violence: Original Sin in Relational Theology*, Continuum, New York, 1995.

7

Overcoming Sin: Conversion and Reconciliation

> The chief sanctity of a temple is that it is a place to which we go to weep in common. A *Miserere* sung in common by a multitude tormented by destiny has as much value as a philosophy. It is not enough to cure the plague: we must learn to weep for it. Yes we must learn to weep. Perhaps that is the supreme wisdom. (Miguel de Unamuno, *The Tragic Sense of Life*)

Nowadays there is a greater realization than ever that one cannot be faithful to the biblical understanding of sin if one does not in the same breath allude to the over-arching context out of which it emerges. That context is first and foremost the story of God's love for his creation and for his people. We have already seen how in the Old Testament this is expressed most definitively in God's attitude of compassion and mercy which maintains and renews the covenant even when people wish to break and destroy it.

All the same, those who critique and caricature the Christian tradition as being obsessed with sin and heavy-handed in its apportionment of guilt to all and sundry may still have a point. Insofar as any approach highlights the evil of sin without being equally emphatic about the mercy and forgiveness which are God's characteristic reaction to sin, it ends up distorting in the same measure the *evangelion* or good news.

For that reason, although the over-riding aim in these pages has been to reflect on sin and on its meaning for humankind today we cannot adequately achieve this task without devoting some space here to understanding the paramount importance and centrality of forgiveness in the Christian story.

The God of the Hebrews established, as we have said, a covenant with his people, and his disposition toward his people was that of a loving parent toward children who were sometimes unruly, ungrateful and unkind. It was an attitude of *hesed*, of mercy, compassion, sympathy and tenderness. God kept to God's promises despite the unfaithfulness and sinfulness of humanity. What is more, this was not merely a sentiment of sympathy: it was a forgiving disposition which readily and concretely translated itself into active love. This love made mercy real and concretely 'demonstrated his love for the helpless and the sinner, particularly in the act of gracious pardon'.[1] The plan of God for his people was the establishment of personal relationships with him and with each other. Even when sin disrupted these relationships he constantly offered his forgiving love to save, reconcile and heal damaged relationships.

Yahweh's will to save was characterized in his *emet* or fidelity to his covenant. He revealed himself to Moses as 'the Lord who is merciful and gracious, slow to anger, and abundant in steadfast love and faithfulness, keeping steadfast love for thousands, forgiving iniquity and transgression and sin' (Exodus 34.6–7; cf. Numbers 14.19; Jeremiah 3.12). Even when Israel's infidelity ruptured the Sinai covenant of love, Yahweh took the initiative for a new and eternal covenant. This in turn was realized, expressed and communicated in the person of Jesus Christ. Because the Word became flesh, human history became God's history.

The Christ event with its climax in the Lord's death and resurrection marked a decisive step in the realization of

God's salvific and reconciling activity. Jesus became the new redeemer. As Yahweh had once brought Israel out of slavery and captivity and guided her to the Promised Land, now Jesus would liberate all of humankind from slavery to sin through his supreme sacrifice on the cross. In the Gospels Jesus is the innocent one, the just one who dies for the injustice of others. He prefers to die rather than to forgo completion of his father's will. He is, in the words of Isaiah, 'the lamb that was led to the slaughter'.

The notion of sacrifice as atonement is, of course, a difficult one. In the Old Testament there was the cathartic practice of the scapegoat ritual. The underlying idea here, as we saw, was the belief that the accumulated sins, infidelities, wrong-doings and violence of an entire community could somehow be transferred onto a blameless animal, which would then atone for these transgressions by carrying them off into the wilderness. As the book of Leviticus demonstrates, a priestly class was to emerge from the people of Israel with the specific task of meticulously offering sacrifice according to detailed and often laborious rites, with the aim of securing atonement for all the sinful deeds that had been perpetrated.

An important corrective to this practice though is to be found in the writings of the Prophets who chastized the people for making animal sacrifices into a meaningless gesture while stubbornly retaining their hardness of heart and obstinacy.

> Enough, though you offer me your burnt offerings and cereal offerings, I will not accept them and the peace offerings of your fatted beasts I will not look upon. But let justice roll down like waters, and righteousness like an ever-flowing stream. (Amos 5.21–4)

And so Yahweh refuses the offerings of sacrificial animals and seeks instead 'the humbled contrite heart' and attention to 'the poor, the widow and the orphan'. Repentance must therefore be real; it must be sincere and expressed in a new and real concern for justice.

A further paradigmatic change is to be found in the New Testament where the saving death of Jesus replaces the atoning practices of the Jewish temple. Jesus becomes, in the words of John, 'The Lamb of God who takes away the sins of the world'. This is not just a senseless sacrifice therefore, it is instead an act of self-offering which is of a piece with the self-donation, the *Kenosis* which were the life of Jesus Christ. 'What makes the life of Jesus a holy sacrifice is the quality and course of his life's work, and the intention to which he gives expression'.[2]

Although Christianity was deeply grounded in and indebted to Jewish tradition there was here a decided change of practice, a 'soteriological shift'. The Son became the victim who pleaded with the Father for forgiveness and mercy. The paschal sacrifice was the Shepherd's gift of his life for the lives of his flock. In this way Jesus demonstrated that sin could only be overcome by faithful love. He was at once, as St Paul explains, both the 'victim' and the 'priest' and it was in virtue of this that he accomplished the salvation of all and put an end to all other sacrificial offerings. An essential aspect of this sacrifice is the pardon or forgiveness of sins. This is not simply about wiping the slate clean or forgetting or even about refusal to seek revenge. It is primarily a gift, as the twin roots of the Latin *per donare* suggests, a gift of the Spirit, which allows the rebuilding and restoring of wounded and ruptured relationships.

Jesus is the personification of Yahweh's suffering servant who 'bore the sin of many and made intercession for the transgressors' (Is. 53.8–12) and by whose wounds we are healed. In this way the merciful love of God is finally and definitively revealed in the Cross of Christ as the unparalleled way in which Jesus loved sinful humanity. 'For our sake he made him to be sin who knew no sin' (2 Corinthians 5.21; cf. John 3.16) and again 'Christ loved us and gave himself for us' (Ephesians 5.2). Similarly, Peter's message before Jerusalem is that 'Christ died for our sins'. In a sense, Christ has 'repaired' human disobedience. Peter himself more than most understood this. His tears as the cock crowed for the third time (Mark 14.72) were an acknowledgement, a physical recognition of Christ's faithfulness when all around had lost faith. They were also to be the basis of his repentance, his renewed faith and ultimately his future leadership of the Church (Luke 22.32).

The post-resurrection appearances are of course a reassurance to the apostles that Jesus, their teacher and master, is risen from the dead; but they are also the privileged and tender moments where they realize that their disastrous lack of faith and fidelity have been forgiven. The events of the trial and crucifixion of Jesus had served to unmask the weakness and fragility of his closest followers. And yet Jesus returns to give them back everything that they thought they had lost. He has foreseen their weakness, their shame and their cowardice and yet he keeps them faithfully and lovingly in his friendship. This attitude toward his humbled and chastened little band of followers is expressive of the forgiveness of a God who gathers all people into his embrace of love. Even the pagans who had a part to play in the judgement and putting to death of the Son of God are thereby also included in the embrace of forgiveness.

This of course had always been Israel's self-proclaimed hope. She had never allowed herself to forget that Abraham's blessing was destined for all people and that the Messiah would one day unite 'every tribe and tongue and people and nation'. This too was to become the basis for Paul's evangelizing and missionary work. 'Christ has died for our sins' was not a narrow sectarian assertion. It was to be instead a proclamation of Good News to all, a confession of faith in the redeeming power of Christ. The formula itself seems to have pre-dated Paul and was probably passed on to him around the time of his conversion and baptism. It is significant in that it is a collective expression of faith. 'For our sins' was the prayer of a community that recognized not only that they had sinned but also that they had been forgiven.[3]

It was a sign also of the collective solidarity that emerged out of the events of the first Easter and out of God's gesture of supreme compassion and forgiveness for his people. Forgiveness had not only a galvanizing but also a reparative and healing or 'making whole' effect. As in the case of Jesus' own earthly ministry (for instance the healing of the paralytic, Mark 2.5–12) forgiveness of sin is clearly linked with healing in the life of the primitive Church. 'Confess your sins to one another' advises James, 'that you may be healed' (James 5.16).

This combination of reparative, restorative and re-integrative effects has come to be described in more contemporary language as reconciliation. The word, however, is deceptive in the modern usage. More often than not it is used to describe the bringing together of warring factions or a meeting of minds between erstwhile enemies. This is patently not the case in the relationship of God to humanity. While human beings may frequently err and stray from the path that they have set themselves, the Father, in contrast, always remains constant and faithful. The sense of the Greek term *katallagé* is of God reconciling all humankind – indeed all of the cosmos – to himself. Human beings are not 'actively' involved in this process; instead they are 'granted' reconciliation. On this point the reformers were right to insist when they underscored the assertion that justification is not the result of human efforts or of the particular merits of the sinner but it is the fruit rather of he who by his 'obedience onto death' won eternal life for all. At the same time one must be careful not to fall foul of what Müller-Fahrenholz calls the 'verticalist reduction' which gives fuel to the privatization of sin that we critiqued in the previous chapter.[4] The Christian tradition has always had a sense that justification is achieved and made real by human beings' co-operation with divine grace and that it doesn't therefore remain purely extrinsic to the human person. The transformation of the person into the image of the Son is a co-operative task. It was for this reason that Jesus opened his public ministry with the clarion call '*metanoiete!*': 'repent and believe in the good news' (Mark 1.15). The joyful good tidings of Jesus' kingdom message are therefore an urgent summons to *metanoia* or a change of heart. The coming of that kingdom in the person, the life, the ministry and the witness of Jesus of Nazareth creates an awareness of the absolute need for God in the human heart. In his earthly lifestyle and life witness Jesus lived out that self-surrender which is characteristic of the eternal Trinity and demonstrated that the destiny of human beings is not to remain apart but to be enveloped by the reality of God. In the Gospels, Jesus' life and ministry are a call to conversion. They are, for all that encounter him, a summons to abandon sin and to turn around, to reorient their life toward the truth and freedom of the kingdom of God as revealed in Jesus Christ.

Already in the prophetic tradition the Hebrew term *shub* had conveyed the sense of a dramatic change of direction, a restoration of familial intimacy and a 'returning home' like the return of the prodigal son in Jesus' timeless parable. This meant that conversion was about the re-establishment of the dialogue of love between God and human beings both individually and in the community. This idea is captured also in the *ruah Yahweh* in the book of Ezekiel, which breathed new life into what had become a bundle of dry bones. The dry bones afflicted by the desiccation of sin were revitalized and raised to new life. The 'change of heart', which the prophets and the psalmists unceasingly call for, is that kind of dramatic event. And yet it is by no means a purely external change. There is always the sense of an intensely personal activity and inner journey, a decisive moment of what Ricoeur calls one's 'existential narrative'.[5]

In modern cardiology a practice whereby an electric shock is administered to a heart with an irregular rhythm is sometimes prescribed. The aim is to stop the heart briefly so that it may re-start on a more regular pattern. In a way the biblical sense of conversion is equally dramatic. It is a complete overturning of one's life; the sinful and disintegrative spiral is jolted to a halt with the aim of reversing the *conversio ad creaturam* toward a renewed *conversio ad Deum*. The dry bones of the moral life must be revived by the breath of the Holy Spirit and by a personal decision of the individual.

If sin is a kind of disintegration and mortal isolation, the return to God ought to be achieved by an effective conversion which restores the order that had been upset and heals the traces of sin. Conversion must be interior therefore if it is to be genuine. 'It sparks up in a man's heart, in the very centre of the personality out of which the sin sprang'.[6] And it can only be 'sparked', to use Anciaux's term, by a genuine contrition – a purposeful regret which acknowledges the estrangement that has taken place from Christ and his gospel. It follows that in order to be Christian conversion must be christological, it must be Christ-centred. To convert does not mean simply to acknowledge transgressions of the Law and to start over. The primary meaning, as Fullenbach has observed, is not so much turning away, leaving behind what is wrong and sin-permeated; it is more about turning around and towards a response to the divine overture of compassion and forgiveness. 'One is asked to let this new, unheard-of-message change one's life, to let oneself be overtaken by this great news and thus to look at reality in a new way.'[7]

Conversion also needs to be total and integral; a recurrent

theme of Jesus' preaching is his rejection of the kind of lip-service about change, which is really only a cosmetic exercise. He severely berates those people whose self-deception is so deep that they cannot see their own need for conversion. He insists instead that there must be a fundamental internal change of attitude, an interior transformation, which is revealed in congruent action.

What we are talking about here is a profound ethical, religious and human experience; it is what Lonergan once described as a 'shift in horizons'.[8] Being a disciple implies repentance and reformation. Unlike the case of many other great teachers, being a disciple of Jesus was not so much about repeating his language and learning his insights and concepts: it was much more about modelling life on his in order to become someone like him. Given that this is so, the death and resurrection of Jesus becomes the paradigm *par excellence* of all conversion. The re-forming and reshaping that is born out of sorrow and suffering allows us to see more clearly the essential relationships of the self to others and to God. After a dramatic change, and initial period of dislocation and confusion, there comes a new focus, direction and meaning in life.

Contemporary psychology has identified four essential moments in the process of conversion. There are:

1. Disorientation.
2. A sense of gathering up the fragments.
3. An experience of mercy and the forgiveness of failures.
4. A sense of the Other, of being as it were 'grasped by God'.[9]

These elements form a classic pattern which charts the 'reversal of sin into forgiveness, of suffering and pain into generous love, of death into life' and which is reflective of 'the law of the cross'. This is what Rahner calls: 'a resolute radical and radically conscious, personal and in each instance unique adoption of Christian life'.[10]

The idea of conversion also gives rise to a further series of questions. Does the term describe a sudden event or a gradual process? It is a once-only experience or may it be repeated? Is this an entirely personal experience of the heart or is there a necessary social dimension? Contemporary theology tries to answer these questions by distinguishing between three types of conversion. In particular it points to the separate meanings of intellectual, religious and moral conversion. This is not the occasion perhaps to rework a question which has been explored at great length and with great technical expertise in the writings of Lonergan, Rahner, Tillich, Erikson and Kohlberg – to name but a few. One can nevertheless affirm that their work in exploring the multidimensional and multi-layered nature of conversion allows for a much more nuanced understanding of the idea today. At one level it can be considered a definitive moment which reshapes and refocuses the entire life of the individual, while at another level it is a process which continues to actualize itself in and through daily life and the normal web of human relationships. Conversion is at once a deeply personal need as well as a moral imperative for communities, people and even nations. It can be described in terms of an event, while at the same time being recognized as an attitude that pervades the moral life.

As well as charting the stages and kinds of conversion, one can also meaningfully speak of conditions of conversion. Perhaps it is this facet of conversion which most clearly illustrates the struggle against sin. The first such condition is simply awareness and admission of sin and guilt.[11] Honesty, truth and a willingness to acknowledge the reality of one's weakness are prerequisites on the path to *metanoia*. 'God be merciful to me a sinner' is the prayer of the publican (Luke 19.9–14) who seeks Christ's forgiveness. It also mirrors the first step of contemporary recovery programmes. The moment of truth is where the addict admits that they are powerless on their own to effect real change and that their lives have become unmanageable. It is a decisive time of acceptance of reality and of the need for assistance from without. The parallel has been adverted to by several theologians who see strong similarities between addiction as a pathological relationship with a substance or process and the idolatry of sin. Both in a real way are constructed on what we have called a false anthropology – a refusal to accept one's own limitations, imperfections and creatureliness.[12] Both involve a 'progressive enslavement' and a vicious circle effect. The experience of being attracted to an elusive and illusory freedom, devastating personal disintegration and isolation, and the self-destroying spiral of deterioration and despair are themes which are common to both the pathology of sin and that of addiction. Recovery likewise in both scenarios entails a commitment to the truth and to an attitude of honestly and is born in that moment of that candid and humble acknowledgement which in clinical terms might be called an admission of powerlessness. In more religious terms one might simply speak of humility before God.

Honesty and candour are the starting points for the individual's process of turning away from sin and returning to the loving presence of God. In analogous ways communities, societies and cultures need to make a decisive break with the sinful past in order to recover collectively from the poisonous effects of sin. In mid-1990s South Africa, for instance, the collapse of apartheid left behind a legacy of distrust and hurt. By way of a remedy the old National Party favoured a Reconciliation Commission, whereas the African National Congress (ANC) sought nothing less than a painstaking investigation of the truth. The resultant compromise, the Truth and Reconciliation Commission, provided a much-needed cathartic process and its very name gave expression to a basic prerequisite for the healing of collective hurt. Similarly, the Church of France, in acknowledging its share of responsibility for wrongs perpetrated during the Nazi occupation, especially those against Jewish fellow citizens, recalled the words of the novelist François Mauriac: 'A crime of this magnitude falls in a not insignificant way on all who were there, on those who didn't cry out and who kept silent for whatever reason'.[13] In like manner, international enquiries into old wounds in Northern Ireland and the Balkans have been important steps along the laborious path to peace in both regions.

By way of support for this approach, Müller-Fahrenholz suggests that there is much more wisdom in the Jewish proverb 'Forgotten prolongs captivity. Remembering is the secret of redemption' than in the popular adage 'Forgive and forget'. He speaks of the 're-membering' in the original sense of bringing together the members and pieces of something that was once complete – a restoration of what has been lost and a joining together of what has been broken. Remembering is therefore a process which calls to mind the deepest convictions and possibilities of people, encourages them to heal forms of dis-memberment and to work toward a better, more integrated society.[14] Confession, admission and acknowledgements of responsibility and ultimately of sin are necessary purgative, purifying and ultimately healing acts.

A second condition is some kind of interior readiness for moral renewal. In an older theological language this would have been described as a 'firm purpose of amendment'. What was meant here was a realization that conversion entailed personal and, on occasions, collective effort to overcome the effects of evil, whether from within or from without. This disposition is encapsulated in the first plea of the Lord's Prayer: 'Thy kingdom come'. It is a plea which first and foremost demands a real personal commitment and engagement. Two things are immediately apparent here. First, on a theological level the wholly gratuitous nature of God's pardon is unquestioned. The Christian understanding of grace has always been thus. The Reformed tradition in particular has insisted that grace comes 'unprevented': it is definitely 'prevenient grace'. The initiative in the reconciliation between God and humanity lies with God alone. The same revelation which gives us an insight into the religious meaning of evil and thus a fuller grasp of the reality of sin also gives us the proclamation of God's commitment to forgiveness and to his faithful and all-enduring love for his people. The sinner nevertheless does not experience himself or herself solely at a spiritual level, for human beings are embodied. The New Testament witnesses to the episode where a paralytic's friends were asked by Jesus 'which is easier to do – to say to this man "your sins are forgiven" or to say "get up, take up your bed and go home"?' would have had no difficulty in identifying the first statement as the easier, for forgiveness is not so readily susceptible of external verification. The episode ends, however, with the paralysed man's mobility being restored. Morally he had already been healed by the divine word of forgiveness; humanly it became much easier to realize this when it found a resonance in his physical cure.

The great tradition of asceticism rests, in large measure, on the same insight. Grace can never be purchased, forgiveness cannot be earned, but neither can one ignore the serious duty of reparation, the need to reconstruct one's own life and the obligation to undo sinful effects in the lives of others. Human beings give expression to the reshaping of their lives in reparative and ascetic acts. There is an inescapable logic in that sin and those effects of sin that are primarily physical in expression should be countered in a physical and tangible way. For en-fleshed human beings it makes sure that the entire human person – body, mind and spirit – should be somehow engaged in the process of conversion. Seen in this way, asceticism is not at all about self-hatred, still less is it about personal feats of endurance or showing 'what one can do for God'. Spiritual 'machismo' can have no genuine point of contact with a gospel of humility and truth. But asceticism does have a very real role in recalling salvation history, and in particular Christ's sacrifice in shouldering the cross so as to defeat sin and complete the will of the Father.

So the practice of penance is ultimately about identification with the cross, even though it may also have a very real human role to play in personal reintegration and in reparation for wrong which has been done. The example of Zaccheus is notable here: 'Behold Lord the half of my goods I give to the poor; and if I have defrauded anyone of anything, I restore it fourfold' (Luke 19.8). What is more, the traditional forms of penance, namely prayer, fasting and almsgiving, show us that the ancient ecclesial wisdom was keen to give penance an orientation toward outreach, concern, and support for others.

This idea of making satisfaction or restoration is paralleled again to a certain extent in the process of recovery from addiction. The 'steps programmes' lead recovering addicts to an awareness of the people who have been harmed as the result of their addiction, to a resolution that direct amends will be made whenever possible. They also insist on the recognition that no recovery will be possible until their lives have been 'surrendered to a higher power'. Here the importance of restitution is not simply that it does justice to those who were initially wronged, but that it also marks a further step in the process of personal acknowledgement and acceptance of responsibility for one's life. The comparison between recovery from addiction and the conversion from sin can also yield two further insights. The first is that both processes involve the entire human person. Like the pathology of sin, the pathology of addiction permeates the whole of human experience and so recovery needs to be holistic and integrative. A resonance may be observed here with those who argue, convincingly for the most part, that the true theological meaning of concupiscence is moral disintegration and fragmentation of human existence caused by sin. Conversion from sin and toward moral coherence and consistency implies by definition an integrative and all-embracing advance. It implies a new focus and cultivation of inner attitudes as well as of patterns of behaviour that bring about changes, which truly heal and make whole again.

A second observation is simply that conversion, if it is to be taken seriously, has to be considered a lifelong task. It needs to be understood as a process and not simply an experience. The recovering addict is under no illusion that recovery is anything other than a lifetime commitment. He or she must commit to an 'honesty programme'. Similarly conversion implies a pilgrim's process of progressive liberation from sin through a gradual increase in sincerity, integrity and candour. Although the experience of and engagement with repentance and reconciliation may be seen as identification with the cross of Christ, it is equally the case that for most people the *via crucis* is not condensed into the space of a few days but is woven instead into a life journey. Recovery from sin and reorientation toward the gospel is therefore for them an integral, organic and permanent task. It is 'the process by which we untie the multiple knots and webs of our cross-addictive sins and progressively integrate ourselves into a new reality'.[15]

Neither is the process capable of being undertaken alone. Recovery requires the simple honesty of confrontation. In the Christian tradition this has long been acknowledged through the confession of sins to a third party where confession is made to one who is entrusted with the ministry of reconciliation and forgiveness. It is also recognized in the centrality of the word of God. It is not one's own fears, guilt or shame (all of which are subject to fluctuation, fixation and indeed manipulation) which in the final analysis provoke contrition and repentance, but confrontation with the message and mission of Jesus Christ. Recovery manifests itself also in progressive reconciliation with other people. Analogously it is to be seen in the efforts made by communities of faith to initiate the process of repentance within themselves. It is borne out also in their efforts to foster the central values of unity, solidarity and respect for creation. Communities of faith, churches and even nations and blocks of nations have therefore a responsibility for integral human development and must also be prepared to open themselves to the same dynamic of repentance, reform and reconciliation. The succinctly expressed aspiration *ecclesia semper reformanda* is a time-honoured acknowledgement that as well as being an individual imperative, conversion is also a shared duty and responsibility.

In their final document at the end of the second Pan-European Assembly held in Graz, Austria in 1997, the Christian churches of Europe clearly recognized this collective and corporate dimension to reconciliation:

> Although we bear the bruises of our lack of reconciliation, we believe that this reconciling power is still at work today among us. It can already be seen in our longing for reconciliation (cf. Romans 8.26f.) and makes us prepared to let our thoughts and behaviour be transformed.[16]

There is here an ecclesiology of the *ecclesia peregrinans*, a faith community which takes as its model the *koinonia* of the early Church, and which sees itself not simply in terms of an institution but as a true *communio* exhibiting genuine regard for all who live in it.

The same document is also at pains to point out that the search for corporate and collective repentance and reconciliation is not about glossing over the very religious, cultural, ethnic and ethical differences which are a fact of life in a multicultural world. Still less is it about whitewashing over the deep differences between the guilty and their victims.

Reconciliation is never a substitute for justice and truth. If separated from these it merely contributes further to sinful divisions and discrimination in the world. True community, true belonging and true solidarity are not qualities that can somehow be bestowed or superimposed in an artificial way. They only come about when people have the space to discover the basic truth of inter-connectedness. The encyclical *Redemptoris Missio* once memorably noted that for genuine dialogue to take place three conditions must be respected:

1. It must be genuinely mutual.
2. There must be no false 'irenicism'.
3. No party must try to impose its view on the other.

The horizontal thrust of reconciliation depends on this kind of candour and honesty and on a recognition of 'the fact of human inter-dependence on a global scale. A realisation of the fact that one's own life and the lives of countless others, whom one may never come to know personally are inter-twined for good or for ill'.[17]

A third and final condition of conversion might be described as openness to the gift of grace. Christian tradition insists that every step to conversion is taken in the light of divine grace. Jesus reassures his followers: 'Ask and it will be given to you: seek and you will find, knock and the door will be opened to you' (Matthew 7.7–8). The invitation that is placed before us is ultimately a call to life: 'I have come that you may have life and have it to the full.' It is an invitation to consciously choose to live and to 'seize the day', to grasp the *kairos* moment. It is also a decision that requires courage. Saying yes to the *Sequela Christi* is in some respects like saying yes to the unknown. It is a journey in faith, hope and love, but it is also a journey where the itinerary is not pre-determined or mutually agreed.

The element of risk is quintessential to discipleship

whereas avoidance of risk smacks of the sinful. In the parable the steward who buried his talent in the ground was described as wicked by his employer because he had closed off all new possibilities including the in-breaking grace of God. Thévenot describes this essential aspect of the process of conversion as the journey from 'idol' to 'icon'. The sinful attitude is idolatrous because it is fashioning of oneself and one's life in the light of and at the whim of one's own needs and desires. It is a narcissistic strategy, which halts the journey and arrests progression toward true freedom by offering an alternative, but ultimately static, goal. Iconic attachment, on the other hand, renders us open to the mystery, to the adventure of discovering God, to the other and ultimately to oneself. It fosters a readiness to be drawn even deeper into the mystery of the One who is the icon of the invisible God, the God whose name is 'love'.[18] This kind of dramatic reorientating and transformation of horizons is very evident in celebrated conversion stories such as those of Mary of Magdala, Paul, Augustine, Francis of Assisi, Blaise Pascal, Paul Claudel and many others.

> Within each individual conversion a new and loving God discloses the world of generosity from which everything originates. Suddenly even what was evil in the past is seen as having led toward a God who forgives. Betrayals are disclosed as wounded trusts; modest faith in the other is refined into a greater freedom to embrace God and neighbour. All of this comes about through the transforming power of conversion'.[19]

Psychologists suggest that the situation is akin to falling in love. Suddenly the world takes on a whole new prospect – what once appeared dull and uninteresting is now charged with interest and with meaning. It is as if one has suddenly found the means to access a whole new universe that was previously unavailable. Where the experience is one of recovery from addiction the contrast may be even more vividly experienced. Deeply ingrained patterns of thought and behaviour, which had kept the addict on a treadmill of self-preoccupation and self-loathing, are gradually replaced with the discipline of honesty and transparency that allows the charting of a new course. Senses that had been inured and deadened are reattained, as the individual emerges from the tunnel of despair into the light of new hope. The power of divine grace erupts in the human heart, the shackles of enslavement are broken, and the journey, which had been abandoned, is once again resumed.

It is recorded that when the creators of the first twelve-steps programmes adopted the neutral, perhaps somewhat insipid language of 'Higher Power' they did so not out of any aversion to Christianity nor even primarily in consideration of those from other cultures and traditions who undertook the programme. Instead, their choice of terminology was above all a recognition that many who suffered from addiction had also suffered alienation and disaffection from God and faith. Yet withal, the thrust of such programmes remains God-oriented, it continues to be a complete surrender of life to the all-powerful, all-loving Other. The baggage of sin, deceit and self-inflicted suffering is left behind and the world becomes a place in which God dwells and reaches out in compassion to all creation.

Consumerism, colonialism, militarism, sexism, racism, sectarianism and terrorism are just some of the collective sinful addictions which have manifested themselves, and indeed continue to manifest themselves, often dramatically, in the world today. For this reason there is a renewed urgency in re-discovering the collective dimension of prophecy. Challenging popular conceptions of pluralism and tolerance and their claim to be moral absolutes will also be an important task if societies and communities are to be persuaded to collectively open themselves to the prompting of Divine Grace. But such profound change is not just wishful thinking, and the dream of solidarity is not utopian. The power of grace is truly transformative, and just as the twentieth century is strewn with examples of man's inhumanity to man so too are there striking examples of that *metanoia*, that change of heart, which brings about new life and new hope.

Another little detail from the recent ecumenical journey of the European churches, in particular a contrast between the circumstances of the two Pan-European Ecumenical Assemblies, graphically illustrates this point. As part of the first such assembly held in Basle, Switzerland in 1989, and by way of a symbolic gesture to show the human spirit's capacity to transcend all man-made barriers, all the participants were invited one morning to go on a short walk in the outskirts of Basle. Since Switzerland, France and Germany meet at the city of Basle, the walk took them through three national frontiers. Some of the delegates from Eastern Europe found that simple exercise so overwhelming that many of them ended the walk in tears. The idea that one could simply stroll through a frontier with a wave of the passport without having to queue endlessly for a visa was incredible to them. That one didn't have to trot back and forward between one government department and another, perhaps having to bribe some officials as might have been the case in their own countries, was too much to take in. This free, almost blasé, crossing of frontiers was, for some, like an impossible dream. Yet in a few short months, as we now know, that impossible dream was to become a reality for almost all the peoples of Eastern Europe. The Iron Curtain was torn open; the Berlin Wall was demolished brick by brick and peoples of Eastern Europe moved freely across frontiers. The two lungs of Europe, East and West, breathed freely again for the first time in half a century.

The gospel insists that dreams can become reality. Sometimes symbolic gestures and celebrations are necessary in order to peel away the mask of sin, to reignite our hopes and to nourish and sustain our visions and dreams.

Notes

1 Tierney, E., *The Sacrament of Repentance and Reconciliation*, Dominican Publications, Dublin/Sydney/New York, 1983.
2 Sykes, S., *The Story of Atonement,* Darton, Longman & Todd, London, 1997, 17.
3 See Guillet, J., *De Jesús aux Sacraments*, Cahiers Evangile, Paris, 1986
4 See Müller-Fahrenholz, G., *The Art of Forgiveness,* WCC Publications, Geneva, 1996, 12ff.
5 Ricoeur, P., *Temps et Récit*, (Ed du Seuil), Paris, 1985.
6 Anciaux, P., *The Sacrament of Penance*, Challoner, London, 1962, 41.
7 Fuellenbach, J., *Throw Fire*, Divine Word, Manila, 2000, 219.
8 Lonergan, B., *Method in Theology*, Herder and Herder, New York, 1972, 235–7.
9 Happel S. and Walter, J., *Conversion and Discipleship*, Fortress, Philadelphia, 1986, 9.
10 Rahner, K., 'Conversion', in *Sacramentum Mundi*, Burns & Oates, London, 1968, 291–2.
11 This is an adaptation of a schema to be found in Peschke, K., *Christian Ethics: Moral Theology in the Light of Vatican II*, Goodliffe Neale, Alcester, 1993; Seabury, New York, 1975, Vol. 1, 332ff.
12 For a fine analysis of these parallels see McCormick, Patrick, *Sin as Addiction,* Paulist Press, New York, 1989, esp. 146–77.
13 Église de France, *Le Repentir*, Desclée de Brouwer, Paris, 1997, 28.
14 Müller-Fahrenholz, G., *op. cit.*, 36–7 and 59.
15 McCormick, *op. cit.*, 186.
16 CEC/CCEE, Final Document EEA2, Christian Commitment to Reconciliation, 1997, 3.
17 Irish Bishops, *Work is the Key,* Veritas, Dublin, 1993, 3.
18 Thévènot, X., *Compter Sur Dieu,* Éditions du Cerf, Paris, 1993, 297ff.
19 Happel and Walter, *op. cit.*, 16.

8

Towards a Synthetic Account of Sin

> We are separated from the mystery, the depth and the greatness of our existence. We hear the voice of that depth; but our ears are closed. We feel that something radical, total and unconditional is demanded of us; but we rebel against it, try to escape its urgency and will not accept its promise . . . Sin in its most profound sense, sin as despair abounds among us. (Paul Tillich, *The Shaking of the Foundations*)

The idea that men and women are morally responsible outside of particular social practices and conventions of praise and blame requires at the very least a conception of someone to whom or something to which they are responsible. To the Judaeo–Christian mind the immediate tribunal before which the self is summoned has always been 'conscience upon which is engraved the law of God'. Norms of responsibility are not therefore to be simply considered a matter of individual choice, or preference, or even social convention. Ultimately the individual is responsible for herself or himself and the demand for an authentic coherent ethical stance is thus fundamental to the moral life.[1]

Ethics in the Christian tradition presupposes therefore accountability, answerability and responsibility. These notions are the means by which we also attribute culpability to persons. William Kneale has noted that moral reasoning 'began with an extended use of debt words' and that the language of debt also 'permeates religious discourse'.[2] Religious debate, in turn, and in particular Christian theological ethics, affirms that the coherence and integrity of life is fundamentally linked to what transcends individual and community life – namely God. This insight gives rise to an 'imperative of responsibility' which in some sense articulates the prophetic call to seek justice, love and mercy and walk humbly before God'.[3]

Responsibility is therefore a core tenet of the Christian faith – responsibility to oneself, to others and to God. This 'expectation of response' as Niebuhr calls it, encapsulates the Christian imperative to turn away from attitudes and behaviour which demean and destroy the integrity of life and to move toward a moral stance which respects, enhances and promotes right relations. It follows then that failure to respond, failure to strive toward right relations, and failure to be fully responsible is of the very essence of sin. This understanding underscores the inadequacy by itself of a 'debt-language' that places too much reliance on those models of law and obedience that tend to characterize and indeed caricature sin in a mechanical, individualistic and actualistic way.

Equally inadequate and unhelpful is the removal of debt language altogether or its replacement with a vocabulary and imagery of fault that relieves persons of all responsibility for their actions. Those psychological, sociological and anthropological approaches that advocate what might be called a 'hard determinism' may succeed in their own terms in lifting the burden of guilt from the shoulders of the sinner. They do this at the cost though of severely diluting our understanding of personal freedom and of rendering the ethical dimension well-nigh irrelevant. Wiping out guilt by wiping out the very identity and self-understanding of the person is, by any standards, a rather crude approach. Besides, it would seem that even in terms of the therapeutic goal the strategy is not an entirely successful one.[4] There is a tension, a tensive quality in the concept of sin, which must be respected and retained if the term is not to be devalued and to lose all currency and meaning. The urge to counter a reductionist or deflated account of sin with an expansionist, inflated but ultimately trivialized understanding, is great but must be resisted. The answer must therefore be a more nuanced and synthetic approach.

That said, an important service has been rendered in disentangling, insofar as that is possible, the separate notions of psychological hurt and moral guilt. One can indeed resonate with Denis Potter's observation that all too often religion was 'the wound and not the bandage'.[5] There are 'guilt laden counterfeits of responsibility', human projections which often do 'colonise religious experience' and have the capacity to damage and distort one's image of God and of self. Theological ethics owes a real debt to the modern sciences for their work in exposing such counterfeits and in highlighting the dangers and deficiencies of a theology of sin which becomes too preoccupied with precise deterrents and precise merits. Sin and its remission can too easily be reduced to some manner of theological calculus. Misguided methods of evangelization and exhortation, which either wittingly or unwittingly inflate the understanding of guilt in order to manipulate it, are ultimately perverting the gospel message of good news and at least to some extent are guilty of producing what Nietzsche called a 'slave morality'.[6]

While it is true that Christianity brings with it a perception of the human being as guilty in its doctrine of Original Sin, this teaching only has relevance in the context of Jesus' liberation of all humanity in his passion and death. Original Sin is therefore essentially about the detection of and 'unmasking of a lie'. The lie in turn, as we have already suggested, is a distorted and flawed self-image which has become internalized and which orients us toward a 'dehumanising self-sufficiency and self-justification'.[7] A wholesome, synthetic account of original sin therefore, far from being at odds with balanced psychological and sociological insights, is in fact engaged in large measure in one and the same project – namely the unmasking of flawed images of God, of self and of the world in which we live. It has been a constant theme of Christian theology from the time of St Paul that divine grace enables us to avoid sin. This implies, however, an acknowledgement of the fact of human wrongdoing, infidelity, selfishness and so forth and of one's accountability for failure. Responsibility and sin are therefore corollaries of each other. In other words, 'to establish the possibility of sin is always simultaneously to confirm the potentialities of human agency and human nature and so, in the final analysis, sin is not an indictment of human nature but a vindication of it.[8] There is a paradox then, an 'inherent irony' in that the very theological concept which more than any other depicts the fragility of the human person and the fragmentary nature of our engagement with the moral life also celebrates the human capacity for change and for the good. This paradox at the heart of the doctrine of sin means that, despite having to grapple with the reality of failure, the teaching bears witness to a very positive underlying theological anthropology.

Viewed in this light it is not altogether surprising that the idea of sin has fallen on such difficult times in the last half-century or so. Modern Western thought has tended to abandon the notion of the *Imago Dei* and with it the idea of the intrinsic worth and dignity of the self. Hans Jonas observes: 'the paradox of the modern condition is that this reduction of man's stature, the utter humbling of his metaphysical pride, goes hand in hand with his promotion to quasi-God-like privilege and power'.[9] Whatever about the centrality or otherwise of this 'will to power', there are two very different and competing theological anthropologies or accounts of humanity at play here. The first one, which asserts the sinful nature of the human condition, seems on the face of it to be a gloomy assessment but is in fact the gateway to an exalted understanding of human persons as created in the image of the three-in-one God. Here, each person is viewed as a unique, distinct and unrepeatable person. Each human being has a personal, existential distinctiveness and because of their personal communion with God each partakes in Being, each is therefore more than their biological individuality.

Unlike the second anthropology, which presents the person as an 'individual', a segment or a sub-division of human nature as a whole, the Christian understanding of person is different in that it 'represents not the relationship of a part to the whole but the possibility of summing up the whole in a distinctiveness of relationship in an act of self-transcendence'.[10] In a remarkable way every man and woman encapsulates in his or her own existence the universality of human nature. And this existence is characterized by freedom and distinctiveness. Each human being is given the invitation and the offer of freedom in love and in personal communion. Each may accept or refuse the offer, which is essentially a choice between going along with the process of being or cutting oneself off from being altogether.

Evidently at the root of these differing anthropologies there are conflicting views of freedom. Modern Western liberal thought has gradually moved away from the idea that freedom may be guided by truth about what is good. Some of the existentialist philosophers (e.g. John Paul Sartre) have for instance put forward an 'ethic of authenticity' where freedom is understood in a radical way, almost as a law unto itself. Sin, in this philosophical outlook, insofar as it has any meaning, is about failure to break the shackles which hamper authenticity – natural law, religious belief and external value systems. To live authentically one must live radically, and if one lives virtuously one does so in the words of Camus only 'by caprice'.

> If there is nothing definitive in nature, no structure in its products, which responds to a purpose, then it is licit

> to do with it whatever one wants, without by this violating its integrity. For there is no integrity in a nature conceived exclusively in terms of natural science in a nature that is neither created nor creative.[11]

The productive and social changes of the last two centuries have vastly multiplied our choices, and with this has come the championing of the right to choose. Someone has described modernity as the transition from fate to choice. Freedom has been exalted as a core value. But freedom is nevertheless elusive and unsatisfying and is too often confused with independence. The result is the relentless pursuit of a phantom freedom that is in fact only a new form of enslavement.

Homo modernus, whether as taxpayer, worker or consumer, is increasingly considered a mere digit, a unit of production, consumption or fiscal reckoning. Emptied of the respect, dignity and indeed of the love due to a person, the human being becomes increasingly viewed as a thing. Man turns into a grain of sand and human society becomes a desert. The relentless pursuit of freedom that severs the 'ties' of religion and off-loads the 'prejudices' of tradition and morality leads only to a mirage. Perhaps part of the wrath and bitterness that was unleashed in sometimes anarchic and violent anti-globalization protests at the beginning of the third millennium was due to this kind of growing disillusionment. There is an increasing realization that grandiose promises of freedom have led not to real liberation but only to the dull conformity of fashion and to the influences of the utterly hollow and ephemeral. In the same way the irony of the Judaeo–Christian stance is that it is an ethic that at first glance appears constricting and even suffocating but which in fact holds out the promise of real freedom.

The key of course is in the acceptance of the human being as essentially relational. Viewed in this light, the ties that really bind us are not bonds of imprisonment at all but bonds of attachment of communion and of love. The freedom we enjoy is a 'created freedom', and therefore the fundamental choice is not really between dependence and independence: it is a decision between a living dependence, which is open to growth and development, and a dead dependence, which refuses to acknowledge our creature status and therefore cuts us off from the source of life.

These competing versions of freedom were also to form the backdrop to the 1994 papal encyclical *Veritatis Splendor* and to the episode of the rich young man's encounter with Jesus (Matthew 19.16–22) which inspired and informed the encyclical's reflections on this topic. Jesus' response to the young man's enquiry about what he must do to gain eternal life was prefaced by a reminder that human good or moral good finds its ultimate source in the absolute good – the 'one who is good'. The aspirations to freedom and to the good are but particular articulations of the desire for the infinite. In this way 'human freedom bursts open to dimensions for which only God is the answer because only the absolute Good satisfies the restless heart'.[12]

Evidently future receptivity to a doctrine or even a sense of sin are inextricably linked to humanity's willingness to remain open to the transcendent. Sin can only be truly understood in terms of the living and personal bond between humanity and God, which is the foundation in turn of all human relationships. That is why 'the second commandment is like the first'. To love one's neighbour as oneself is, above all, to respect the freedom that he or she holds from God. As Paul explained in his image of the 'Body of Christ', each member of the living organism develops freely so long as it is intimately joined to the rest of the body. So the foundation for the injunction to love one's neighbour as oneself is the intimate relationship and relatedness of human beings. I love you not because you are giving me this or that, but because in a certain sense I am you and you are I in communion with our common source which is the triune God. This is the idea that is the common focus, the synthesis and the regulating centre of all our individual freedoms.[13]

If such are the philosophical and theological underpinnings of the Judaeo–Christian account of sin it should also be acknowledged that it has been the genius of the same tradition to propose side by side with the formal doctrine of repentance a tradition of sacrament, ritual and religious practice. This has provided another means by which to understand and to concretely experience the mystery of sin and conversion. Recourse is made here above all to the language of symbol, metaphor and bodily enactment (which is the language of Scripture after all) in its attempt to embrace in a holistic and accessible way the human experience of wrongdoing, repentance and reorientation. In more recent times this kind of indirect language has attracted the attention of philosophers such as Paul Ricoeur and Réné Girard who have shown how symbolic and mimetic communication can speak beyond logic to the human heart. In particular they have drawn attention to what Ricoeur calls the 'double intentionality' of metaphor, that is the literal and latent layers of meaning.

Symbols and metaphors give rise to a 'spontaneous hermeneutics', a struggle toward newer and fuller levels of meaning. This insight has led to several attempts in recent years to revitalize and re-energize the theological language of sin by re-examining the underpinning imagery. More particularly, these theological initiatives have sought to shift the emphasis away from juridical/criminal models which tend to reinforce a highly individualistic anthropology toward more therapeutic and communitarian paradigms which successfully evoke the universal struggle with the crippling and disintegrating power of sin.[14] These approaches are at once more coherent with the wider scope of biblical wisdom and more receptive also to the interdisciplinary, synthetic approaches that are found in recent theological debate and research. But they are only useful insofar as they are tolerant of the actual blend of metaphor and imagery, which emerges from the scriptural and doctrinal tradition. There is no one paradigm or metaphor that holds the definitive key to the understanding of sin. Each must dialogue, modify and, as Ricoeur puts it, 'struggle' with the others. Any attempt to underplay the 'juridical' model for instance would be just as misconceived and misguided as the well-documented tendency to overplay it formerly was.

Among these theological voices the contributions of those writing from the political, ecological, liberationist and feminist perspectives have also been very much to the fore. While feminist theologians have tended to concentrate less on the theme of sin and more on the patriarchal identification of women with sin, their work has on occasions lucidly demonstrated how prone our religious imagery and theological paradigms are to distortion and bias. Such bias they contend may also express itself in ethical theory and in the basic understanding of the moral life. Spiritual and moral machismo, for instance, may be found in inordinate preoccupation with victory over individual sins to the neglect of responsibility for nourishing and nurturing relationships.[15] Some critiques go much further and argue that there is a tendency within traditional conceptions of morality to legitimate so-called 'feminine virtues' thereby actually perpetuating injustice and oppression. Whatever the validity of these claims, there is no doubt that feminist thinkers have done a great service in highlighting the 'sin' of sexism. The blatant dishonesty at the root of a 'belief that gender is the primary determinant of human characteristics, traits, abilities and talents and that sexual differences produce an inherent superiority of a particular sex'[16] has been exposed for once and for all.

This theological critique also raises questions about the accuracy of *hubris* as a type for universal sin since this very concept 'mirrors chiefly the experience of men' who aspire to positions of power and influence.[17] But perhaps this criticism implies a too facile identification between *hubris* and the traditional Judaeo–Christian conception of sin. The latter, as we have tried to point out, was more concerned with an integral account of human sinfulness, of which *hubris* was but one expression. To be sure, the classical theological conceptualization of sin has its limitations. Nevertheless the underlying understanding of sin as a negation of who one truly is called to be rendered this theology at least potentially open and receptive to new experiences of sin such as those evoked today by those who reflect feminist, ecological and social concerns. What is more, there would seem to be some validity in the arguments of those who suggest that the notion that 'men sin through pride and women through weakness' is itself a stereotype which has become a little dated at the beginning of the third millennium.[18]

Even so, patriarchal structures and sexist attitudes are still a reality in society generally and in Christian churches and communities more particularly. Like liberation theologians, feminists have drawn inspiration from the central prophetic tradition of Judaeo–Christian ethics which emphasized God's defence of the oppressed, as well as the need to criticize oppressive power structures in society and the importance of recognizing ideological elements in religious belief. They have also critiqued an overly spiritualized account of original sin that fails to respect the 'earthedness' and bodiliness of human life. Reuther argues:

> The Big Lie tells us that we are strangers and sojourners on this planet, that our flesh, our blood, our instincts for survival are our enemies. We have fallen to this earth and into this clay through accident or sin. We must spend our lives suppressing our hungers and thirsts and shunning our fellow beings, so that we can dematerialise and fly away to the stars.[19]

It is one thing to acknowledge with Augustine that 'we have here no abiding city'; it is quite another to use this an excuse for avoiding the individual and societal responsibilities which are an essential part of our human calling.

But feminists such as Reuther do see within the tradition seeds of a new way of imaging God, sin, conversion and so forth. They point to the maternal love and compassion of Yahweh, the presence of Wisdom conceived of as a feminine reality, and the as-yet under-developed female imagery associated with the work of the Holy Spirit. Although there is a great variety and divergence of opinion and of intensity among feminist reflections on sin, one senses here a thrust toward a more fully human and inclusive understanding of fault and finitude. Construed in this way the universal sinful tendency 'consists essentially in denying the co-humanity of the others one experiences'.[20] Such reflections have made an invaluable contribution to unmasking the dehumanizing side of sin. In doing so they are broadly at one with theologians who argue that sin is essentially about refusing the invitation to play our part in the human family's journey towards becoming more fully human.[21] The fact that Christian theology, and in particular its reflection on sin and evil, has until very recently been constructed predominantly by men, to the near exclusion of the experience and insights of women, inevitably means that there is essential corrective work to be done. Only thus can theology itself hope to be freed from the dehumanizing effects of sin.

At the same time, a new awareness of the fragility and delicate ecological balance of the environment has led to increased reflection on the human duty of stewardship for all creation and what this means in terms of concrete individual and collective moral responsibility. Here there are ready parallels with the classical Christian view of justice as right relationships. Sally McFague explains: 'If the most basic meaning of justice is fairness then from an ecological point of view justice means sharing the limited resources of our common space.[22] Ecological sin is quite simply then refusing or neglecting to share these resources with those who are most in need of them. It is also a failure to recognize the inherent goodness of the natural world. That goodness is a deeply rooted conviction throughout Scripture. After each of Yahweh's acts of creation the creation accounts recall that 'he found it very good' (Genesis 1.31). Similarly the Psalms proclaim that 'the earth is the Lord's and all that is in it; the world and those who live in it, for he has founded it on the seas, and established it on the rivers (Psalm 24.1–2).

There is a pervasive recognition here that the world is not ours and that human beings are a part of the created world. Made in the image and likeness of God, human beings are to reflect God to the rest of creation, to look after and care for the world and its natural resources. There is the implication here of a caretaking role, a duty of stewardship, which is part of a grace-filled respect for the integrity of all creation. Such an attitude is directly opposed to the purely utilitarian stance, which considers natural resources to be expendable and disposable commodities. It is also a relational attitude, an attitude that calls for a rediscovery of our connectedness to and dependence on the earth. This sense of justice toward all creation had once found expression in the ancient Jewish tradition of the Sabbath law and the Jubilee Year. There was a sense of allowing the earth to replenish its resources and restore its energies during a fallow period. For theologians like McFague, Dorr, McDonagh and others, traditions like these bespeak a practical and ethical wisdom, which understands that the relationship between the earth and human beings, like the relationship between persons, must be one of mutual giving and receiving.

Failure to respect this mutuality and reciprocity is a failure to act honestly and is therefore sinful. 'A land ethic that aims to preserve the integrity, stability and beauty of the biotic community is an example of living appropriately on the land and refusing to live the lie that we are the conquerors, the possessors and the masters of the earth'.[23] One can speak meaningfully therefore of ecological sin and of the need to encourage awareness of sustainability issues. *Sollicitudo Rei Socialis* argues for a greater realization of 'the limits of available resources and of the need to respect the integrity and the cycles of nature', as well as the 'mutual connection in an ordered system, which is precisely the cosmos'.

Reverence for the earth is an ethical and religious imperative that touches our self-understanding in a profound way and which asks searching moral questions of our individual and collective lifestyles. Insofar as we refuse to recognize these questions or reject their import or fail to answer them in an adequate way, we also disregard the perennial summons to 'act justly, love tenderly and walk humbly with our God'. This rejection is what we have learned to call sin.

The fields of political theology and liberation theology are the locus of some other recent attempts to contextualize the concept of sin. As with the ecological and the feminist perspectives, one cannot do justice to the breadth of industry and scholarship being undertaken in these fields in a brief *tour d'horizon* such as this. In large measure the preoccupations of these theologies though are the same ones we that have already adverted to in scrutinizing 'social sin'. 'Political' theologies such as those of Johann Baptist Metz and Dorothee Sölle have sought to develop theological reflection on sin and guilt in the context of contemporary social relationships in the modern world. Their approach sets out specifically to challenge and critique the individual bias, which is a part of modern Western culture. Metz's theology was influenced by his traumatic experiences of the Second World War. He and Sölle raised the question of the suffering of innocent victims and of the large groups of people who are denied the opportunity of becoming 'subjects' due to political and social repression. According to them, there is a need for people to liberate themselves from the structures that impede their integral growth and development. What is required is a collective conversion, an 'anthropological revolution' where people emancipate themselves from the influences of 'privatism' and from the sinful tendencies of consumption and domination. This can only be achieved when collectively we are prepared to leave behind the competitiveness and egotism of our 'success ethic' and to realize the full implications of our status as essentially social beings. According to this view we must commit to an acceptance of responsibility for ourselves, for the human family and for the world.

> When Christianity takes its place in the movement towards the development of world-wide community it will be able to express, in and for that great community, its understanding of a solidarity that is free from violence and hatred.[24]

It is not hard to see how so-called political theology became the forerunner of so many contextualized theologies in the latter half of the twentieth century that were to lay great emphasis on the 'primacy of praxis' and the search for universal justice. That said, despite the radical tone of this approach there is also recognition here of what Metz calls the 'eschatological proviso'. This is an acknowledgement that God's promise of salvation will never be fully realized within history and that only the 'God of the living and the dead' ultimately can fulfil the promise of history.

Western political theologies were to provide much inspiration for liberation theology, especially in their critique of a 'privatized ethic' that only camouflaged the true causes of sin. Many of the liberation theologians went for a distinction between social sin and individual sin which had social repercussions. They tended to do this by pointing to the differences between sin understood as 'communal', that is pertaining to the interpersonal dimension of primary relationships, and as 'societal' sin, which concerned the more complex, impersonal and structural secondary relationships. The human being was therefore at the nexus of a set of two-way mutually impacting relationships, each of which was vulnerable to the damaging and destructive effects of sin.

Advances in human, political and economic science also provided the opportunity for a penetrating analysis of each of these relationships, thus bringing them into the theological foreground. In this way society's mechanisms were laid bare with the birth of the social sciences. They teach us that poverty, hunger, ignorance, misery don't just happen but are the demonstrable results of socio-economic and political relationships.[25] And so liberation theologies argued for a social prismatic in all theological accounts of sin that would serve as a necessary antidote and corrective to a too privatized moral climate and culture. They placed the poor at the centre, as those who most embodied the hope for change and liberation. They also reworked the great biblical motifs exemplified by the Exodus event as well as the New Testament emphasis on Jesus' compassion toward the poor. This they saw as only underscoring the importance of liberation in Christian life. In other words, liberation had to be seen in concrete, practical and tangible, as well as spiritual ways.

The sheer multiplicity of views within the liberation perspective makes any general comment on their theology of sin quite difficult. At one level it is but a reflection of the broad post-conciliar trends toward a renewed appreciation of the dignity of the human person and of the demands of social justice and is therefore advocating a more thorough and integral understanding of sin in all its dimensions. At another level some of its more radical exponents have been accused of substituting political salvation in history for external salvation and of underplaying 'the full ambit of sin whose first effect is to introduce disorder into the relationship between God and man and cannot be restricted to "social sin"'.[26] In any event, liberation theology has unquestionably been instrumental in the repositioning of theological emphases from the universal to the particular, the privileged to the deprived and the systematic to the narrative and performative.[27] It has drawn much-needed attention to the disastrous human suffering caused by unjust institutions and structures, and has urged humanity, and especially faith communities, to take a responsible rule in fighting injustice and building solidarity. Perhaps it is here though that the advocates of social sin, understood in the 'hard' sense, are on their weakest ground. If one is really to urge responsibility in social justice one must be prepared first to acknowledge the facts of responsibility and accountability as human possibilities and realities, otherwise the same determinisms which explain way sin will just as surely erode the very grounds for social action and responsibility.

If there is a common strand or unifying theme in the so-called contextualized theologies it is their insistence on sin as opposition to Jesus' message, where the kingdom is no mere extension of intrinsic human possibilities but a radical restructuring of inter-human relationships grounded in justice. What is more, this justice is not simply about corrective action or redress for wrongs that have been done; instead it is truly restorative and re-creative. Sin is understood as nothing less than the rejection of God's plan for filial and fraternal relationships, while justice on the other hand 'concretises the praxis of love and so realises the Kingdom'.[28]

In this optic there is room for much common ground between classical and contemporary theology because each in its own way presents sin as the human failure, whether individual or collective, to be what one is called to be and to realize the fullness of one's individual potentialities. A more dynamic understanding of creation and of the human person can thus allow the classical and the contemporary views to speak meaningfully to each other.

It is here perhaps that the personalist and process perspectives are at their most valuable. While Boethius' definition of the human being as 'an individual substance of a rational nature' has proved a timeless insight and has become the bedrock of much ethical reflection and rights language and legislation, it does not capture in itself the fullness of the Judaeo–Christian concept of the person. In particular it fails to do justice to the 'dynamic nature of human existence, with its movement toward the fulfilling of aims or goals'.[29]

One thinks here of Amos' concept of justice as represented by the river gently growing deeper and flowing toward the sea, of the case of an incremental line of advance and progression throughout the moral life. Perhaps there is a sense too in which the moral life may be seen as a task of becoming human, a task in which one is called to co-creator with God. One is invited also to accept responsibility for one's life, and to gradually realize agapeic love both in one's own person and in communion with others. Understood in this light, sin is, above all, the failure to incarnate love and to co-operate with God in a great act of giving birth to a new *koinonia*. The re-creative, regenerative process takes place first and foremost in the human heart, and all that is required is the co-operation of human free will – the willingness to surrender one's aspirations to self-sufficiency and to accept God's love and the implications of that love in outreach to others.

This dynamic and synthetic view of creation and of the human person sees the *Imago Dei* as at once gift and task. Each human being has been created in the image and likeness of the triune God and is therefore conferred with an undeniable dignity, but each is also called to make real that 'communion of love' which is the hallmark of the same triune God in his or her own life. This is the awesome but also potentially tragic adventure of human nature. Sin therefore represents one possible expression of that freedom which is ultimately 'a refusal, whether small or great, of human destiny in its noblest reach'.[30]

Columbanus, the great Irish pilgrim monk, and author of a penitential handbook, once suggested in one of his sermons that each human being may ultimately determine the 'picture' that is to be painted in and through their lives. 'Let us not be the painters of another's image . . . for righteousness and unrighteousness . . . are opposed to one another. Then lest perhaps we should import into ourselves despotic images let Christ paint his image in us'.[31] According to this view the moral life works gradually either to confirm the imprint of the *Imago Dei* upon one's entire being or else to slowly replace it with the image of the tyrant – to whom or to which one has become enslaved.

Even in these earliest theological reflections there was evidence of a synthetic, integral and holistic approach. There was also keen awareness of the continuous as well as the immediate aspects of moral behaviour. Indeed, it has also been the tenor of the vast learning and practical wisdom of the Christian tradition to regard both the immediate and continuous dimensions as co-essential aspects of the moral life. In other words, one has to allow each of these dimensions to co-exist in a creative and complementary tension.

Recent theology has therefore sought to root its reflections on sin in a more adequate synthetic and integral understanding of the human person. It has rediscovered the dramatic and incredible assertion at the heart of Matthew's account of the final judgement that 'as often as you did this to one of the least of these my brothers and sisters you did it also to me!' (Matthew 25.31–46). To love others is therefore to love God, and conversely to fail others is to fail God. Sin is therefore not only a moral fault it is also a religious failure. Recovery from sin challenges us in turn to a renewal of faith to a renewed acceptance of the fact that the path away from sin and toward healing and wholeness cannot be travelled alone. Growth out of sin is but another way of describing our own personal part in the ongoing story of humankind as it continues its struggle toward the realization of the kingdom of God.[32] It is here too that the lament for sin and the sadness of the contrite heart become a joyful sorrow. For in truth we are only able to mourn and lament when we really appreciate what we have lost. A genuine grasp of the 'reality of sin' becomes therefore the first moment of our encounter with God. This is the moment when we truly discover the awesome extent of his love.

Notes

1 Schweiker, W., *Responsibility and Christian Ethics*, University Press, Cambridge, 1995, 73f.

2 Kneale, W., 'The Responsibility of Criminals', in James Rachels (ed.), *Moral Problems: A Collection of Philosophical Essays*, Harper & Row, New York, 1971, 172, cited in Schweiker, *op. cit.*, 75.

3 Schweiker, *op. cit.*, 133.

4 Karl Menninger's *Whatever became of Sin*? remains a remarkable insight and stimulating essay on the importance of sin beyond the strictly religious and theological worlds. See Menninger, K., *Whatever Became of Sin?*, Hawthorn, New York, 1973.

5 See Potter, D., *Seeing the Blossom*, Faber, 1994, 5, cited in Phillips, D., 'Exposing the Wound: A Christian Reflection on Guilt', *Downside Review,* 1999, 408.

6 Nietzche F., *On the Genealogy of Morals* (Trans. W. Kaufmann), Vintage, New York, 1989.

7 See Kelly, K. T., *New Directions in Moral Theology*, Chapman, London/NY, 1992, 120f.

8 McKenna, J., 'The Possibility of Social Sin', *Irish Theological Quartely*, (60), 1994.

9 Jonas, H., 'Contemporary Problems in Ethics from a Jewish Perspective', in *Philosophical Essays*, Prentice Hall, 1972, 172, cited in Schweiker, *op. cit.*,73.

10 Yannaras, C., *The Freedom of Morality*, St Vladimir's Press, New York, 1996, 21f.

11 Jonas, H., 'Dalla fede antica all uomo tecnologico', *Il Molino,* Bologna, 1991, 263, cited in May, W. E. 'Veritatis Splendor: An Overview' Communio, 1994, 21.

12 May, W. E., *op. cit.*, 23.

13 Tribon, G. *et al.*, *Christianisme et Liberté,* Arthéme Fayard, Paris, 1952, 7ff.

14 See, for instance, McCormick, P. T., *Sin as Addiction*, Paulist Press, New York, 1989; my own *The Irish Penitentials*, Four Courts Press, Dublin, 1995; O'Kelly, K., 'The Changing Paradigms of Sin', *New Blackfriars* (November 1989) and Cronin, K., 'Illness, Sin and Metaphor', *Irish Theological Quarterly*, 61, 1995.

15 See Gilligan, C., *In a Different Voice*, University Press, Harvard, 1983, 19f.

16 Coll, R. E., *Christianity and Feminism in Conversation*, Twenty Third Publications, Connecticut, 1994, 112.

17 Scherzberg, L., *Sünde und Gnade in der Feministischen Theologie*, Mainz, 1990; see also Van Heijst, A., 'Sin as the Disruption of Relationships', in F. Vosman and K. W. Merks (eds), *Aiming at Happiness*, Kampen, 1996, 141.

18 See Carmody, Denise L., *Christian Feminist Theology*, Blackwell, Oxford, 1995, 113.

19 Reuther, R., *Sexism and God-Talk*, Beacon Press, Boston, 1983.

20 Cahill, L. S., *Sex, Gender and Christian Ethics*, Cambridge, University Press, 1996, 118.

21 See, for example, Daly C. T., *Creation and Redemption*, Gill and Macmillan, Dublin, 1988.

22 McFague, S., *The Body of God*, SCM, London, 1993, 116. NB: I have relied here extensively on McFague's excellent presentation and analysis of ecological sin.

23 McFague, *op. cit.*; see also Leopold, A., *A Sand County Almanac*, Oxford University Press, 1949, 224–5.

24 Metz, J. B., *Faith in History and Society*, Seabury, New York, 1980.

25 Moser, A. 'Sin as Negation of the Kingdom', *Theology Digest* 30:1, Spring,1982, 29.

26 Congregation for the Doctrine of the Faith, *Libertatis Nuntius*, Catholic Truth Society, London, 1984, 14.

27 See McDonagh, E., 'An Irish Theology and the Influence of Particulars', in *Irish Challenges to Theology,* Dominican Publications, Dublin, 1986, 102–29.

28 Moser, *op. cit.*, 28.

29 Pittenger, N., *Cosmic Love and Human Wrong,* Paulist, New York, 1978, 13 – an excellent essay on the implications of process thinking for the doctrine of sin.

30 Pittenger, *op. cit.*, 44.

31 *Sermon XI.*

32 See O' Kelly, K., 'Saints or Sinners? Towards a Spirituality of Growth Out of Sin', in *From a Parish Base*, DLT, London, 1999, 166.

Index

Alagartes (Syrian goddess) 9–10
Anciaux, P. 132
Aquinas, St Thomas 55–7, 80, 86, 89
Arendt, Hannah 85
Aristophanes 9
Aristotle 6–7, 13, 18, 45, 73
asceticism 137–8
Asclepius cult 8
Athanasius 44–5
Augustine 48–51, 57, 70, 80, 85, 86, 90, 98, 115, 142, 157
Azor, John 59

Babel, Tower of 21, 22, 23–4, 100
Babylonian concept of sin 3–6, 15, 26, 84, 85
baptism 59, 78, 90, 91

Caesarius of Arles 48, 52
Camus, Albert 151
Celtic Christianity 15, 51–4
Chardin, Teilhard de 87
Chrysostom 46
Cicero 11
Clement of Rome 43
Columbanus 52–3, 54, 164
consumerism 94–6, 143
conversion 80, 131–45
  and social sin 115, 117–18, 121–2

Didache ('Instructions of the Apostles') 42
Donne, John 41
Druidism 13–15
dualism 12, 49
Duns Scotas, John 57

early Christian church 39, 41–51
Eastern Europe 144
ecological sin 157–9
Eden myth 21, 22, 24, 25, 51, 85, 86, 87–8, 89–90, 104
Egyptian concept of sin 1–3, 15, 26
Epic of Gilgamesh 84
Euripides 6, 9
Evagrius 47–8
evil 83–6, 87
  choice between good and vi–vii, 46, 56, 68, 79, 85
  concept of in early civilizations 1, 3, 4, 16, 17, 84
  and the Eden myth 88
  Greek apologists on 45, 46
  in the Judaeo–Christian tradition 18
  metaphysical 83
  in the New Testament 34, 35
  in Pauline theology 76–7
  and social sin 116–17

feminism 155–7
forgiveness of sins 39, 43, 125, 130, 132, 137, 139
France, Church of 135–6
free will vi–vii, 46, 56, 68, 79, 163
freedom 66, 67, 69, 94, 151–3, 163–4
  and moral choices 72–4
  and self-sufficiency 96–8
  and social sin 115, 118–19
Fuchs, J. 74
Fuellenbach, J. 109
fundamental option theories of sin 77–9

Gaudium et Spes 67–8
Girard, Réné 154
Gnosticism 16
God
  and the Eden myth 87–8
  love for his creation 28–9, 30, 68, 70, 109, 125, 126, 165
  and personalism 69–70
  Yahweh 21–5, 27, 28, 38, 126, 127–8, 157, 158
Good Samaritan parable 110, 111, 123
Gospels 29–35, 38, 49–50, 104–5, 127
grace, and conversion 136–7, 141, 143
Greek apologists 43–8
Greek concept of sin 6–13, 15–18, 45, 84, 85
Gregory the Great 47
Gregory of Nissa 45
guilt and sin 1, 6, 7, 30, 85, 87, 92–3, 94, 149–50
  social sin 114–16
Gula, R. 78

Hades 8
Hegel, G. W. F. 86
Heidegger, Martin 92
Hermas Mand 42–3
Hesiod, *Theogony* 84
Hippolytus 44
Holy Spirit 33, 37, 39, 68, 71, 121, 132, 157
Homer 7, 8, 9
Huxley, Aldous 63

Ignatius of Antioch 43
Ignatius of Loyola v
Irenaeus 68
Irish monasteries, penitential systems in 51–4
isolation and insulation 97–8

Jesus Christ 18, 29–35, 41, 89, 103, 153
  and conversion 131
  death and resurrection 126–7, 128–9, 133, 138
  and love 32–4, 38–9, 63–4
  and parables of mercy 31–2
  people raised from the dead by 49–50
  and social sin 103, 105, 108–9
Jews 5, 84–5, 126, 128, 158
John Paul II, Pope 114, 119
John, St 34–5, 80, 85, 88–9, 108
  and social sin 119–20
Jonas, Hans 150
Julian of Norwich 109

Kant, Immanuel 87, 100
Kierkegaard, S. 92
King, Martin Luther 103
Kneale, William 147–8

Latin American Catholic Bishops' Conferences (CELAM) 113–14
Leibniz, Gottfried 83–4
Levinas, E. 107
liberation theology 159, 160–2
Lonergan, B. 133, 134
love
  God's love for his creation 28–9, 30, 68, 70, 109, 125, 126, 165
  of God 70, 73, 93
  'Great Commandment' of 64–5, 66
  and the moral life 93–4, 94–5, 163, 164
  of neighbour 64, 70, 73, 153–4
  and personalism 99–100
  teachings of Jesus on 32–4, 38–9, 63–4, 65
  teachings of Paul on 37–9
Luther, Martin 57–8, 90–1

McFague, Sally 157–8
Mackey, J. P. 93
Marcus Antoniius 13
Mauriac, François 136
Mausback, Joseph 63
Maximus the Confessor 111
Menninger, Karl vi
Metz, Johann Baptist 159–60
Mithraism 10
moral character 73–4
mortal sin 75–6, 79, 80
Mounier, E. 99
Müller-Fahrenholz, G. 130–1, 136
Mystery religions 7–8

New Testament 29–39, 35–8, 41, 71, 89
  Gospels 29–35, 38, 49–50, 104–5, 127
  and liberation theology 161
  and the social dimension of sin 103, 108–9
Nietzsche, F. 100–1

Ockham, William of 57
Oedipus 1, 45
Old Testament 21–9, 26, 27, 38, 48, 71, 125
  and conversion 131–2
  the 'Great Harmartology' 21–4, 100
  and liberation theology 161
  Prophets 28, 103, 127
  and repentance 126, 127–8
  and social sin 103, 104
original sin 58, 59, 60, 86, 91–2, 149, 156
Orphism 7, 8–9, 16

Pan-European Ecumenical Assemblies 140, 144
Pascal, Blaise 72, 83, 86–7, 100, 142
Paul, St 35–8, 48, 49, 67, 68, 76–7, 85
  and *anomia* 33
  and reconciliation 129–30, 142
  and social sin 105–6, 122, 123
  and Stoic dualism 12
penitential systems 43, 51–4
Persae of Aeschylus 6
personalism 69–76, 99–100
political theology 159–60
Potter, Denis 149
'privatization of sin' 106, 117, 118, 131
Protestant reform movements 57–9, 90–2, 137
psychology
  and conversion 133
  and sin vi, 66, 92–3, 94–5

Rahner, Karl 74, 76, 133, 134
reconciliation 51, 135–7, 139–41
responsibility 66, 69, 147–50, 162
  in early civilizations 1, 16
  and social sin 108, 115
Reuther, R. 156, 157
Ricoeur, Paul 87, 112, 123, 132, 154
ritual sin 26–7, 29
Roman Catholic Church 59–60, 77
  and original sin 91–2
  Second Vatican Council 63, 67, 112
  and social sin 112–14, 115, 116, 119

sacrificial rites 5, 9, 17, 25, 27, 127
Sartre, Jean-Paul 151
Schilling, Otto 63
scholasticism 50, 55
Schoonenberg, P. 100, 105, 119
scriptural account of sin 21–39, 103–9
Segundo, J. L. 103
self-sufficiency 96–8, 163
Seneca 13
Sermon on the Mount 30–1, 72
social sin 103–23, 162
Sölle, Dorothee 159–60
Sophism 7, 9
South Africa 135
Stoicism 7–8, 10–13, 16, 50, 84
structural sin 112, 116, 120
synthetic view of sin 78–9, 147–65

Tacitus 44
Tertullian 44
Theissen, J. P. 95, 96
Theophilus 44
Thévenot, Xavier 89, 142
Tillich, Paul 147
Tillman, Fritz 63
tragedy, classical Greek 16, 23, 45
Trent, Council of 59, 91
triplism, Druid doctrine of 14
Tübingen School 63

Unamuno, Miguel 125

venial sin 75, 76, 79
vices, Evagrius' list of eight generic malevolent thoughts 47–8